END-TIMES
simplified:
preparing your heart for the coming storm

David Sliker

forerunner
BOOKS (F)

Kansas City, Missouri

ForErunnEr **BOOKS** (F)

End-Times Simplified: Preparing Your Heart for the Coming Storm
By David Sliker

Published by Forerunner Books
International House of Prayer–Kansas City
3535 East Red Bridge Road
Kansas City, Missouri 64137
(816) 763-0200 Ext. 675
www.IHOP.org

ISBN: 0-9776738-0-4

All Scripture quotations are from the New King James Version of the Bible. Copyright © 1988 by Broadman and Holman Publishers, Nashville, Tennessee.

Cover design by Benjamin Voran
Interior design by Dale Jimmo

Printed in the United States of America

Dedication

This book is dedicated to my bride and dearest friend, Tracey Sliker. My greatest hope is that our life together would be like unto a love letter that moves the heart of a King.

TABLE OF CONTENTS

END-TIMES
simplified:

Foreword

One of the first questions the author of this book asks is, "Why study the End-Times?" It's a great question. There are many reasons all Christians should study the End-Times and this book does an excellent job of explaining what those reasons are and why studying the End-Times does not have to be a confusing thing.

My own Christian journey was not one focused on the End-Times until about four years ago. The whole topic seemed fearful and irrelevant to me for the longest time. Once I began to search the Bible for information about the topic and ask God to give me insight about it, however, I discovered that I have a God-ordained role to play in God's plan for the End-Times. You do too. We all do. Studying the End-Times is critical for every believer, and getting connected to God's heart regarding the topic is essential for the time in which we are living.

Jesus instructed us to "watch and pray" in Mark 13:33. Jesus was calling us to be ready, to be prepared for one of the most exciting times in human history. The Scriptures are full of information about the End-Times and are actually quite clear about the return of Jesus. It is one of the most written about topics in the Bible.

David Sliker has broken down this topic so anyone – even the person who has never even thought about the End-Times – can understand what is happening now and what will happen in the future. Using clear language and an informal writing style, he has simplified a topic that so many have complicated. I want to assure you that understanding the End-Times is totally manageable for everyone and anyone. This book will go a long way in helping you get your mind around the events of the End-Times and what the future holds. God has gifted David with a sharp intellect and given him much understanding about how human history will play out according to the Scriptures.

This book is part of a series of "Onething Reality" books. The goal of the "Onething Reality" book series is to provide foundational biblical teaching on topics that are essential to every Christian's life in God and the core realities of Onething Ministries. As a ministry of the International House of Prayer Missions Base, Onething Ministries shares the same core values and realities of IHOP-KC and publishes "Onething Reality" books as a means of sharing those core values with the Body of Christ.

David and his wife, Tracey, each play an important part at the IHOP-KC Missions Base. David is an instructor at the Forerunner School of Ministry and oversees our personnel department. Tracey directs our One Thing young adult internship program. I so love her zeal for this generation. They have three great kids and my family loves the Sliker family. David and Tracey are real gifts to us here at the IHOP Missions Base.

I encourage you to read this book with an open mind and an open heart and to ask God to speak truth to you as you do. I pray that you will find answers to many of your questions and be inspired to seek the Lord more about the End-Times. More than that though, I pray this book will leave you with a burning desire to see the return of Jesus, for the study of this topic is all about we, the Church, being ready and longing for His return.

Dwayne Roberts
Director of Onething Ministries
International House of Prayer Missions Base
Kansas City, Missouri

END-TIMES
simplified:

Prologue

Eschatology literally means, "the study of the last things." It is the study of the End-Times, the period in history before the Second Coming of Jesus Christ. It is a challenge to write a book about the End-Times, not because studying the End-Times is difficult, but because it can be difficult to communicate the truth of God's Word when people have various, complex views and preconceived notions about the Bible and what it says. Ideas or interpretations become lodged in a person's mind, and it can be problematical for them to think of particular Bible verses differently. We all need help from the Holy Spirit to understand the Bible because our unrenewed minds are incapable of grasping much of what the Bible says without the Holy Spirit's assistance.

Despite the difficulties and obstacles to communicating about and understanding the End-Times, it is vital that all believers study eschatology. There has never been a time when understanding the End-Times was more critical than now, because many agree we are living in the days long prophesied, the "beginning of the end." Like the sons of Issachar, "who had understanding of the times, to know what Israel ought to do" (1 Chr. 12:32), there is a unique invitation to this generation to plunge into the Word of God and devour its contents in regard to the End-Times. Fortunately, it will be easier for those living through the End-Times to understand them. Such people will have a perspective that past generations did not have. Even now, the events about which the Bible speaks are unfolding before our eyes. Jesus is waiting for people who will decide to lay aside the reasons why they shouldn't study the End-Times and instead ask Him to help them do so.

The fog of confusion many people feel hovers over the Bible can be lifted with hunger and prayer. This book is an invitation to begin a journey into the study of the End-Times. Those who embark on this journey will discover God's magnificent end-time and eternal plan for them and for all believers. They will fall more in love with God as they ponder the glorious return of a King like no other and His triumphant victory over darkness. Jesus is indeed a King like no other, and He is looking for modern-day prophetic messengers willing to study the End-Times and prepare the Church for the time of His return. The greatest realization of all, however, is that mankind's journey does not end with Jesus' return. Our journey continues into eternity, where we will go with Jesus on an adventure that thrills our hearts and satisfies our souls forever. This eternal, joyful and magnificent journey can begin today for those who are hungry for more of Jesus.

END-TIMES
simplified:

Why Study the End-Times?

I remember sitting through many lectures on eschatology as a college student and I remember fighting to get through them. I cared about two things: passing the course and moving on to what I perceived as higher and greater things in life and ministry. After graduating from college, I became a youth pastor, and the extent of my vision was to mobilize youth to love Jesus and evangelize a few of their friends in the process. My biggest dreams involved seeing dozens of youth spending the rest of their lives in full-time ministry. I wanted to inspire young people to serve the Lord with all their hearts. The longer I labored, however, the more I was confronted with my limitations as a man and as a minister of God. As I came face to face with my limitations and the limited impact my ministry had, I became hungry to see the manifestations of God's power about which I had often heard. These explosions of power always seemed to happen somewhere else to someone else, and leave lasting impressions on hearts and minds. I wanted God to show up to my little group of friends. So with a little zeal and lots of idealism, I organized prayer meetings for youth and young adults with only one thing on the agenda: revival.

We met regularly. We hungered for God to come in a way that seemed just out of reach. We were always desperate for God to answer our prayers for revival, but never sure if we would see it. We reached for what we thought was a high vision: hundreds of youth and young adults swept into a wave of revival power. The number in my mind was in the thousands, if I dared to confess my ambition.

Then a strange turn of events suddenly expanded my simple hopes and dreams into something more. I found myself on staff at the International House of Prayer in Kansas City, Missouri. It was there that I discovered promises truly worthy of the God who is more wonderful and glorious than we could ever imagine. And it was there that I embarked on a journey with my friends and co-laborers to discover what the Bible had to say about the End of the Age.

Like children on an Easter-egg hunt, we dove into Bible passages that in the past I had barely skimmed. I discovered parts of the Bible I hardly knew existed, and passages I hadn't realized were relevant to my generation. What I found in those passages shocked me, and transformed my understanding of the God I serve. They expanded my perspective of the times in which I live. Over time, even "common" passages took on a new and fresh air of exhilaration. My heart became more and more alive at every newly found discovery.

As I became consumed by this exploration into the depths of the Word, I realized that something great and unbelievably terrifying is about to happen, maybe even during my lifetime: the Second Coming of Jesus Christ. God has written and is bringing to pass a drama worthy of His signature and wants each of us to take part. The challenge is preparing for what will come.

It stunned me to find that I could contend in prayer for something far beyond revival, something that will affect the entire world. The return of Jesus will be the most glorious event in history, and will be the fulfillment of all our hopes and dreams in God. At the end of all things, at the end of the darkest hours of human history, He will come. When He comes, He will come to a Church experiencing her finest hour, a Church manifesting the greatest maturity, power and authority the world has ever seen. The events the Bible describes are breathtaking. They are staggering in their scope and might. At the heart of this currently unfolding drama is a God who has planned great twists and turns for the End of the Age. What He has planned from the beginning of time will top anything the creativity of the entertainment world could ever conceive.

Who can imagine God exerting His will in such a way that the strength of all the nations will be completely shattered? Who can imagine that in the wake of the greatest trauma in human history, Jesus Himself will step onto planet Earth, having been set into place by the Father as ruler over all the nations? Who can imagine the manner in which God has chosen to bring to pass such events? God's chosen method is that of fervent prayer being lifted up to the heavens night and day, birthing the age to come. The manner chosen by God is one in which His people gather in humility and weakness to pray for the return of Jesus and cry out for true justice to come to Earth. God is leading His people into intimacy and a lifestyle of intercession, which will lead to prayers full of longing for Jesus to return and full of love for God and His perfect plan. The intercessory prayers of the Church will come into agreement with the intercession of Jesus and the Holy Spirit. The Church will have a loyal, wholehearted desire for union with Jesus. The result of all the prayer will be His return. Jesus the God-Man will split the sky in answer to the prayers and intercession of the believers on Earth.

Jesus' motivation is desire. In His heart is an indescribable longing, a deep yearning, for true intimacy and unity with each one of us. It is hard to imagine that the reason for the shaking and trouble to come is the inner fire that burns in Jesus to be with us. In what manner will we be "with" Him? What does it mean to be with Him? True intimacy has been defined by Jesus, the One who fully understands love in its fullest sense. His divine activities on Earth must be examined through the lens of what it truly means to be with Him and walk with Him in the age to come. I sometimes pause in wonder when I consider the nature of the union that awaits each of us in the Kingdom of God, which will come in fullness to Earth. The nature of our coming union with Jesus is rooted in a love far beyond anything we have experienced or imagined. The practical outworking of that love and what it looks like is awesome to consider. Scripture is filled with pictures of life with Jesus after His Second Coming.

Our efforts to discover the reality of Jesus' perfect leadership and His desire to be with us is the study of the End-Times. This reality awaits the hearts and minds of the hungry, who long for more than information or heated theological arguments. Studying the End-Times means discovering the way Jesus is moving, planning, strategizing, stirring, calling, inviting, praying and waiting patiently. Men and women move ever forward into the depths of their wickedness, seemingly at odds with the dream in the heart of the Great Shepherd. Jesus is unmoved, however, and fully committed to God's plan. The nations are rightfully His; and they will be fully His, despite the plans of His enemies, who even in their opposition, are doing exactly what must be done for that plan to come to fruition. We cannot appreciate the full beauty and glory of who Jesus is until we discover how brilliantly He leads. Once we begin to uncover the mysteries of His plans for each of us, we cannot help but fall more deeply in love with Him. He does everything He does to be with us.

So why study the End-Times? First, there is no better way to gain insight into the brilliance of Jesus' leadership, to discover what He cares about most, and to come to love His methods, ways and divine activities. We may know intellectually that His thoughts are higher than ours, but often we are content with simply having that information, and never explore how or why or what those thoughts might be. As we give our time to studying the End-Times, we will come to know Jesus as we never have before. He wants us to know Him as much as we can, and He wants us to *want* to know Him as much as we can. We are able to draw nearer to Him and know Him more intimately than we think possible, but in order to do so, we must be committed to pursuing the knowledge of Jesus above all other pursuits.

②. Second, there are many passages in the Bible about being prepared. Again and again in Scripture, prophets, messengers and apostles sounded an alarm to the people of God: "Get ready!" It is clear the events that happen before Jesus' return will be more intense and troubling than anything that has happened or will happen again (Matt. 24:21). The Bible is clear in its description of the terrifying and destructive events and judgments that will take place. These judgments will exact a terrible toll of lives. Many people wonder why this must be. Will it be because God is angry? Because God is desperate for vengeance? No, neither of these is true. God is kind and tender and loves mercy, and it is out of His great love for His people that He will bring to pass these things the Bible describes so graphically. We should study the End-Times so we are ready for what is coming, so our hearts and minds are prepared. If we are prepared, we will run to Jesus with confidence when all Hell breaks loose on Earth, not away from Him in terror, as many will do (Luke 21:26).

So, the best way to get ready is to fully embrace the pursuit of knowing Jesus better, which is accomplished by spending more time with Him and in His presence. Knowing Him and being with Him make our hearts different. We have less fear, doubt and insecurity, and more confidence, trust and stability. This inward transformation only comes from living a life of prayer, which is simply talking with Jesus and being in His presence; and studying His leadership style, personality, thoughts and emotions. Only if we become grounded in Him in a way that produces confidence, trust and stability in us, will we have the strength to stand steady when everything else crumbles around us. As we prepare, there is a secret agenda for each of us stirring and boiling deep in the heart of Jesus. He plans for each of His believers to actively lead and point others to Him in those days. He doesn't desire for us to simply survive or escape the End-Times, but for us, as His close and loyal friends, to lead people to safe ground and salvation in the midst of them.

(3)   The third reason to study the End-Times has to do with reward. When Jesus comes, He will bring His reward with Him. Those who have been faithful in their given charge in this age will receive the fullness of their reward in the age to come, when Jesus rules the nations of Earth. To be faithful in our given charge requires knowing what our charge is. Knowing what our charge is can only be discovered by cultivating intimacy with Jesus and reading the Word of God. We know from the Bible that the new believers in the early Church faced conflict, hardship and persecution for living what were perceived as radical lifestyles. In the Bible's epistles, we read that the leaders of that new movement, the apostles, brought comfort and encouragement to the new believers by reminding them of their coming rewards.

The perspective of the apostles in almost every letter of the New Testament is one rooted in and looking forward to another age. Their perspective is linked to the call to complete obedience in lifestyle as it relates to the judgment and reward that accompany that future age. They knew a divine secret, and were called to share it with other believers: the reward given by King Jesus will be related to the life we live before He comes. Faith birthed by God in our hearts leads to our salvation, but from that moment forward, we are judged and evaluated according to our works (Rev. 22:12). The works that matter to God are diligence and obedience, which cause meekness and humility to grow within us. He cares about partnering forever with meek people to accomplish great things. We choose at the moment of our salvation to join a heavenly family. We then choose what we will do for the rest of our lives as part of this family.

This incredible truth is meant to motivate us, stir us, awaken us, and poke at our complacency and self-satisfied pride. It is meant to open our eyes to the broader reality that there are plans moving rapidly into place for the revolution that will bring disruption to every institution on the planet. Jesus will come to take over the world, and He wants each of us to have a place of honor next to Him. He wants to give *everything* to us, a prize beyond anything for which we could have prayed or imagined. He will not give us the full reward if we simply pray prayers of confession and need, and then live self-centered lives of indulgence and self-interest. The reward He has for each of us will be given in love to reward our authentic love – not just the emotion of love, but the kind of love that produces diligence, faithfulness, obedience, humility, tenderness, kindness, endurance and compassion. Real love causes us to voluntarily change the way we relate to the One for whom we profess our undying love. Changing the way we relate to Jesus in turn allows us to have a richer, fuller relationship with Him. Real love for Jesus will receive its ultimate reward when He returns.

All three reasons for studying the End-Times are inseparably linked because of the way God brilliantly leads our lives. To give ourselves passionately to knowing Him is to read and meditate upon His Word and commit to a life of prayer and fasting. When we do, we take seriously what we read in the Word. To find Jesus in His Word is to discover what is most important to Him. More than anything else, Jesus really, really wants to come to Earth, far more than He wants us to come where He is. He longs to take the nations of the Earth as His inheritance from His Father (Ps. 2:7-9). To discover and agree with His deep desire, however, we must confront a problem most people don't want to talk about; we must face a dilemma most people want to hope is either an imaginary idea or a crisis that will affect someone else.

The dilemma we must face is that the great and terrible Day of the Lord, which the Bible says will shake the entire planet, will probably come sooner rather than later. The problem we must confront is people's reluctance to contemplate and prepare for this day. Earth is currently filled with people who are unaware of or unwilling to think about the coming trouble. The truth is the trouble will come, and those who are not ready for it will be overtaken and swept away by it. This great storm will wash away the ones who are vacationing, partying and celebrating, trying to make sense of their lives in ways that will never bring sense or order. If they press on daily in their vain and empty pursuits, endlessly focusing on comfort and better lives and happy endings, while completely ignoring the God who will come to reward love and punish sin, they will not stand. The end for many will not be happy.

In the End-Times, even some people in the Church will find themselves in the same dilemma as those who are unsaved: unable to stand. It doesn't have to be this way. Jesus did not die on the cross for us, only to have us abandon Him in offense. He was not bruised for us so we could escape our own struggles and trials. He died and rose again so we would be awakened, as Paul said in Philippians 3:8-11, to the "excellence of the knowledge of Christ Jesus." According to Paul, who suffered the loss of "all things" for Jesus (Phil. 3:8), there is no greater calling in life than experiencing great glory *and* pain that we might know Jesus. Paul's reasoning was, "if, by any means, I might attain to the resurrection of the dead" (Phil. 3:11). Paul wanted two things out of life: to reach with all His might to know King Jesus, and to receive the full reward the King would bring with Him when He returned. Jesus has promised both things to all believers (Rev. 22:12).

To study the End-Times is to make a deep resolution to discover what our present and future King is like. It also is to make a firm resolution to ready ourselves for His Second Coming by doing what needs to be done in our lives so we are prepared to serve with Jesus as His diligent friends. Finally, it is to make a whole-hearted resolution to reach for the full reward He wants to give us. As we do, we will be motivated to live a life that reflects the values of Jesus and honors His ways. We must decide to make our lives about more than busy activity that produces little fruit. We must focus on more than just talking about what to do and how to do it. We must strive to have our lives be authentic expressions of what Jesus had in mind when He saved our souls from death. He laid hold of each of our lives for a reason, and He desires that we, like Paul, would want to lay hold of that reason with all our strength.

END-TIMES
simplified:

CHAPTER ONE:

The Bible Was Written for Everyone

A few critical issues should be addressed before seeking to understand God's heart regarding the End-Times. For those new to this subject, these issues often come to mind immediately and can be boiled down to two questions. The first question is commonly, "Can I study and even understand what the Bible has to say about the End-Times?" It is followed closely by the second, "How do these passages of Scripture apply to my life?" Some feel biblical prophecy is too difficult a subject for them. Some lack the motivation to wade through what they view as mostly irrelevant passages in the Bible. Some feel many sections of Scripture contain no information to help them better serve and love God today. Some view studying the End-Times as a hobby for which they don't have time because of what they need to do today, in the here-and-now.

In studying eschatology, or any other biblical topic for that matter, we need to change how we approach and relate to the Word of God. It is common to approach the Bible from a self-centered, needs-based perspective, using the Word of God as some sort of self-help or self-improvement manual. If our normal mode of Bible study revolves around only what is important to us in our daily lives, we tend to view the Word as nothing more than a problem-solving tool. It becomes no more than a source to which we run for encouragement when we feel sad or troubled. If this is our approach to the Bible, prayer is often simply a search for personal comfort and a means for overcoming obstacles. Fasting then seems to us a strange, unnecessary exercise, a quirky relic of the ancient fathers of the faith. While the Bible does help us and give us encouragement, and prayer does bring comfort and help us overcome obstacles, they are both about so much more. And when we understand more about the "so much more," we see fasting as both a necessary and desirable practice.

The good news is right now God is bringing about a change in the Church's understanding of all these practices. There is a shift taking place globally, especially among young adults. God is sparking hunger in them and stirring them to reach for more than easy answers and self-help philosophy. God is awakening a desire in them that motivates them to make lifestyle changes before God and man. He is encountering them in a way that produces radical passion for Him and a yearning to experience the highest heights of His love. This consuming inner fire is driving them to seek the heart of God with a rare, single-minded determination. Perhaps like no other time in history, growing numbers of young people are embracing a lifestyle of prayer and fasting. Throughout history, there have been outbreaks of revival connected to regional pockets of people praying and fasting. There have been small gatherings of young adults who clung to the heart of God and, through prayer and fasting, birthed revival and transformation in cities, towns and lives. Could it be the Holy Spirit is stirring and awakening a prayer movement to contend for revival on a larger scale? If so, to what end?

The simple answer would be a large-scale revival breaking out all over the world, a revival larger than any previously documented. God loves revival, but even large-scale revival is not God's highest or final goal. There is something more. There is something beyond even the greatest of revivals, for which He wants us to contend and fight. While we may feel unable to fathom what that something might be, the answer is astonishingly simple: the Second Coming of Jesus.

The Church in general has been passive about this event, but the Second Coming of Jesus has always been at the top of the agenda in the courts of Heaven. The first- and second-century believers were consumed with the return of Jesus. They would be shocked to know His return is not the primary thing on our minds today. Many differences between the earliest generations of Christians and the recent and current generations of Christians are due to this difference in focus. Today's Church has for the most part dismissed the Second Coming as something entirely dependent upon the whim of God, an event that will take place whenever He decides it is the right time for it to take place. How odd it would seem to most modern Christians to walk into a church and find its main focus to be the Second Coming.

As odd as that may seem, however, there are churches with such a focus, and God is orchestrating a change of perspective among both Christians and non-Christians. One of the top-selling book series of all time is the *Left Behind* series, which presents a fictional account of the End-Times. A recent *Time* magazine cover story documented the increasing American obsession with the end of the world and Armageddon. More people are thinking about eschatology today than we might think. More people are wondering about it than have since the first century, at least according to the number of people buying books on the topic. The statistics indicate the number of people today seeking understanding in this area far exceeds the number of people doing so in the first-century Church. The question is not whether people are thinking about the End-Times, but why they are thinking about the End-Times.

The relevance of studying eschatology increases significantly when people believe they might be living in the End-Times. Biblical prophecies become far more interesting when we consider the

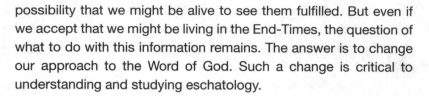

possibility that we might be alive to see them fulfilled. But even if we accept that we might be living in the End-Times, the question of what to do with this information remains. The answer is to change our approach to the Word of God. Such a change is critical to understanding and studying eschatology.

The Bible Can Only Be Understood by the Hungry and Thirsty

Consider Paul's words in 1 Corinthians 1:27: "But God has chosen the foolish things of the world to put to shame the wise, and God has chosen the weak things of the world to put to shame the things which are mighty."

Some people struggle with reading the Bible because they feel they lack the intelligence to grasp its complexities and depth. The Bible, however, was never intended to be the realm of only the intelligent and the learned. It was written to be read and understood by everyone. It is meant to be the source of life, where all people can let their imaginations run wild and enjoy the deep waters of God's heart, as well as learn about the complex mysteries and plans of God. When anyone receives heavenly wisdom from God, that wisdom is of a different age and on a higher level than human reasoning. Such "higher wisdom" often frustrates and confuses those who are "wise" by the world's standards. It offends those with self-seeking minds. It is a total mystery to those who are "lovers of themselves," as the apostle Paul called them, and to those who elevate self-preservation above all else. Such "wise" people are like the Jewish religious leaders described in Acts 4, who confronted Peter and John about their preaching. Those men possessed some of the sharpest minds in the Roman Empire. They were brilliant intellectuals who had risen to the top of a culture of educated men. Still, these wise men were frustrated, shocked and offended by the heavenly wisdom from the mouths of two "uneducated and untrained men."

What was remarkable about Peter and John, according to

these religious leaders of the Sanhedrin, was simply that it was obvious to all "they had been with Jesus." Our greatest problem in comprehending the Word is not the Word itself, or our lack of intellect, but our lack of true intimacy with Jesus. We can't possibly understand words sprung from the heart of Jesus if we do not really know Him. We can't possibly relate to Him on an intimate level if we don't love Him the way He loves us. The words and passages are indeed confusing to those who are distant from God. Paul said the Bible is foolishness "to those that are perishing" (1 Cor. 1:18). Our lack of comprehension is directly proportionate to our distance from God and His heart. Intelligence will never bridge that gap; intimacy with Jesus will.

Gaining knowledge and having the capacity to retain more of it, will never be enough to help us comprehend the Bible. Those who are the wisest by the world's standards often use their vast knowledge and logic to accomplish self-centered, self-preserving and self-serving goals. Men and women rich in worldly wisdom put their minds together and create world systems that empower sin, grant permission to wickedness, and establish webs of deception that entrap hearts in empty pursuits. James 3:13-16 reveals the truth of God: the results of even the greatest exercise of man's reason are confusion and the convergence of "every evil thing." Those who are wise according to the world do what seems right in their own eyes (see Judg. 21:25; Prov. 12:15), because their own way seems more attractive than the mandates of the Bible. Such people often read the Bible and embrace one or two teachings or principles that agree with their personal philosophies of decency and kindness, and reject the rest as irrelevant fables and fanciful stories. According to King David in Psalm 2, all those who rule the nations will completely reject the Bible in the days to come.

The way of the Lord is to make the truth of the Scripture accessible to anyone who sincerely wants it. If we set aside time daily to read and pray through the Bible, its secrets will be opened to us. The time we devote to something reveals the extent of our hunger for it. God has placed in each of us the keys to unlock His Word. Ecclesiastes 3:11 says that God "has put eternity in their hearts," which means He has placed in us a longing for Him and for His truth. This inner longing for eternity is the hidden desire in the heart of every man and woman to know his or her Creator. This yearning, this hunger, is a gift from God and is meant to stir us to ask. "Ask, and it will be given to you; seek, and you will find; knock, and it will be opened to you" is the promise given by Jesus in Matthew 7:7.

We must ask Him to help us understand. Our minds are untrained and unrenewed (Rom. 12:2), and by nature our hearts are dull and unresponsive to the invitations of the Holy Spirit. As such, the Word seems a foreign thing to us, its language of another age, and its truths of another reality. Because the reality of the Bible is so different from the one in which we live, we can be fooled into attempting to wrestle it into submission to our existing culture and systems of thought. But the truth of the Bible stubbornly resists our efforts with its exceptions to our rules, and eventually we are forced to approach the Bible with contrition and humility. It overcomes us with its strength. Man cannot conquer the Bible; it will always conquer us. It forces us to ask for help in deciphering its mysteries.

When we finally surrender, not laying aside our intellect, but comprehending the manner in which the Bible surpasses it (Eph. 3:19), we are then free to turn to the only methods proven to unlock the Bible: prayer and fasting. We ask the Lord questions in prayer. We fast, knowing that voluntarily weakening our physical strength awakens in us deep spiritual hunger. We pray for understanding (Eph. 1:17) and the revelatory gift of the Holy Spirit to know the heart of Jesus. We ask what motivates Him and what stirs Him. These questions birth more questions, and we become driven to search out the Scriptures to find the answers. Hunger increases as understanding comes. It consumes us over time, until we can find nothing better to do with our time than read, sing, discuss, ponder, meditate upon and study the Scriptures. God becomes fascinating to us. He captures our attention.

The end-time mysteries, the strange prophetic declarations, are not too hard for us to grasp. We can attain understanding and wisdom through God's gift of hunger. When we decide we want to unlock the Bible, God is delighted, because He wants to allow us to unlock the deep places of His heart, even more than we want them to be unlocked. He wants us to know truth and discover mysteries far more than we want to know and discover. God can't wait to show us answers to our questions, so He can share with us in the joys of discovery, the "wow" moments that knit our hearts to His. The more frustrating our pursuit, the more satisfied we are with attaining truth. God's ultimate goal is to do far more than simply give answers, though. He is after our hearts. He wants our time, affections, attention, hopes and dreams, and He has set up a brilliant way to capture and then consume us with desire for "more!" of Him. It is the joy of asking, the pain of hunger, the internal burning of thirst, that drive the desperate to ask, seek and knock; and just at the moment our frustration seems unbearable, He opens the door. Living water fills us. We get far more than an answer to a question; we receive life in our inner-most beings.

We can take courage in knowing that understanding the Scriptures is possible for anyone. It is the destiny of every true son and daughter of God. The Scriptures we find baffling will make sense in time. The question isn't, "*Can* we understand?" It is, "How badly do we *want* to understand?"

An Appeal for a Bible That Means What It Says

Hunger for interpretation is the most helpful instrument in Bible study, but we must be diligent to take the Word of God at what some scholars call "face value." Other scholars make the same appeal, but instead call readers to a "plain-sense" (or common-sense) meaning of the text. Whichever phrase scholars choose, they are all calling believers to recognize that the Bible means what it says. This is not an appeal to take all passages literally, for when interpreting the Bible, it is important to bear in mind each author's intent and style. Figurative statements are meant to be understood as such, as are literal ones.

The symbols and poetry in many of the Bible's end-time passages can be intimidating, so it is important to remember that, just as understanding the Bible is not limited to the intelligent, neither is it limited to those with degrees in Greek and Hebrew or to those who can afford numerous study aids. Tools such as commentaries, concordances, and Bible dictionaries are valuable in Bible study, but are not indispensable. Comprehending the mysteries in the heart of God is unavailable only to those who have no hunger. Satan's strategy from the beginning of Church history has been to use any means necessary to deny people access to the Bible. One of his chosen methods in our day is subtle intimidation. He attempts to convince the Church that much of the Bible is too symbolic or too complex to be understood by most people.

The truth about Bible symbolism is that there is far less of it than we think. And often the symbolism in the Bible does not negate the literal nature of what is being described. For example, the artifacts and furnishings of the Tabernacle of Moses and the Temple of Solomon described in the Old Testament were literal objects that really existed. They also had symbolic meanings beyond their physical functions, and were thus both symbolic and literal. Exploring the symbolic meaning of literal things enables us to better grasp God's redemptive purposes for them. The symbolism of the objects always pointed to a deeper reality.

Another example of symbolism is found in Chapter Four of Revelation, written by the apostle John. John described the vision he had of the throne room of God. What he described is not just a symbolic glimpse of God's throne room, but a very real description of God's very real throne room, which really contains a throne on which sits the One who is like jasper and a sardius stone in appearance, and which really has an emerald rainbow around it.

While the external beauty John described is awesome to ponder, all the elements of that beauty are also symbolic of a deeper reality. Think of it this way: when a person smiles, the smile itself is a real expression, but the external beauty of the smile also gives a picture of, or symbolizes, what is happening within the person's heart. With both God and man, internal realities have external expressions. In the case of John's description of the throne room, the jasper radiance speaks of God's brilliant, undefiled purity; the sardius speaks of the fiery, burning passion fueling His emotions; and the emerald rainbow speaks of His tender mercies toward us.

Taking the Bible literally often pushes us into a frustrating pursuit of understanding. We may feel as though certain passages could not possibly be true in light of what we *think* we know about God and His nature. When some encounter difficult-to-swallow passages, they over-symbolize them, and discount the literal meaning when it offends their sensibilities. They rationalize that certain passages must be symbolic because they can't accept that they mean what they say. Take for example Revelation 19:11. Many think Jesus couldn't or wouldn't possibly return on a real horse, so they dismiss the description as symbolic. Many don't want to think Psalm 110:5-6 means Jesus will really execute the heads of nations and fill up the roads with dead bodies after His return, so they choose to interpret it as symbolic and meaning whatever conforms to their image of who Jesus is supposed to be.

God's promise to all believers is that the verses we find most troubling when taken literally, will make sense as we pray, fast, study and spend-time with Him. It is the common sense meaning of the Scriptures that stirs true fascination with God, not someone else's symbolic interpretation of those Scriptures. When we have an intimate connection with the end-time plan of God, the passages begin to come alive and make sense. The possibilities of understanding and knowing God become endless as He moves us beyond our notions of what we think *should* be into the realm of what He knows *can* be. When we believe God is big enough to fulfill His prophetic plans as literally as they are described in His Word, He will become to us more awesome, more glorious and more beautiful.

The Question of Relevancy

Once people conclude that they can understand the Bible, they raise the question of its relevance. If we accept that it's possible to understand the Bible, and in particular its end-time passages, we may next wonder if and why it is pertinent to do so. We question what is to be gained or accomplished by doing so. However, studying the End-Times becomes relevant when we realistically consider the current state of the world in light of what the Bible says will happen in the End-Times. Anyone who studies the End-Times will realize that it is quite possible that Jesus will return in our lifetimes. Studying the End-Times become considerably more relevant as this real possibility sinks in, and we begin to radically change course and alter the way we live our lives before God and man.

Some believers are comfortable with the possibility of Jesus' return and the end of all things, as long as these events remain nebulous "maybes" that don't disrupt their lives. When the possibility of Jesus' return in our lifetimes upgrades to a probability, the End-Times and the Second Coming of Jesus become disruptive forces in our lives. Scripture passages pertaining to His return take on new meaning. Believers begin to feel a new sense of urgency and take far more seriously the Scriptures about preparation and lifestyle. Everything in our lives is challenged, as we wrestle with doubt in the backs of our minds, even though we believe that He is coming sooner rather than later. Our life choices seem strange when contrasted with those of "normal" people striving for greater normality. Pressure to dial down our new convictions regarding the End-Times and our lifestyles comes from the most unlikely sources. In the midst of this struggle and as a result of our increased feelings of urgency, however, a focused, ever-growing prayer life emerges.

When probability upgrades to a living conviction in our hearts and minds, the question of relevancy and the question of whether prophetic passages, particularly those in Revelation, are relevant to our lives, cease to be issues at all. We begin to live based on our conviction that the Book of Revelation was inspired by God, and given to us as a clear warning of days soon to come. When we have a personal conviction that He is coming very soon, whether in our lifetimes or the lifetimes of our children, our hearts are gripped by a certainty both frightening and risky. It is frightening because the events of the End-Times will be frightening. But it is risky because the issue of the End-Times is controversial. Other people have made end-time predictions and ended up looking foolish and having lost their credibility. Fear of being wrong is as haunting as the fear of what some would call "irresponsible scholarship." We wonder if it is irresponsible to hold such strong convictions about such a volatile and divisive issue, particularly when, according to some, every generation of believers thought Jesus would return in their lifetime.

Much has been written about the perspective of the first generation of believers, who seemed convinced the Lord would return in their lifetimes. From the strength and forcefulness of some of Paul's exhortations regarding their lifestyles in light of Jesus' coming, it appeared those believers lived in the "definitely" camp, not the "possibly" one. It seemed all the signs were in place for the return of Jesus, particularly given the speed with which the gospel was spreading across the Roman Empire. It seemed the return of Jesus in their generation was certain, as it seemed entirely possible that the gospel of the Kingdom would reach "the ends of the earth" (Matt. 24:14). In fact, at that time, the remaining of Jesus' twelve disciples had scattered themselves to the far reaches of the known world for that purpose.

Then something catastrophic happened that led to a change in the thinking of the first- and second-generation believers. Jerusalem was destroyed in 70 A.D. after a failed Jewish revolt. The city, which had been under siege for two years, lay in ruins. The great Temple, a source of national pride and the seat of Jewish worship, was completely destroyed, brick by brick, just as Jesus had prophesied (Matt. 24:2). Suddenly, all of the promises in the Torah that pointed to a glorious Israelite kingdom ruling the world in prosperity and victory seemed impossible. Then, in 135 A.D., after a final Jewish rebellion against Rome, Jerusalem was wiped off the face of the Earth. There was no longer an Israelite kingdom to rule anything.

As the years unfolded after this tragedy, Church leaders began to write of the end of the world as an event that would take place far in the future. Many did not know what to do with all of the passages in the Bible that involved Israel, a nation that had ceased to exist, and began interpreting those passages symbolically. Persecution eventually stopped, and the Church became a legitimate institution in society. The signs of the times appeared to have changed, and the world seemed headed for glory rather than judgment. Those in the Church seemed to accept that Jesus would not return in their lifetimes.

This mindset prevailed for the next 1,700 years of Church history. Believers no longer thought much about the End-Times. The letters and books of Church leaders and theologians from every generation of believers provide insight into what was on the minds of people in each generation of Church history, and it wasn't the End-Times. Instead, rising conflicts over doctrine and the person and nature of Christ dominated the conversation for much of the next few centuries. Symbolic interpretation became the dominant characteristic of Bible study and writing because of various influential schools of thought. Catholicism in Western Europe competed with Greek Orthodoxy in Eastern Europe for influence in the courts of kings and rulers. In later centuries, Church practices and their impact on the nature of salvation led to the Reformation, but the reformers had no more use for the Book of Revelation or eschatology than their predecessors. Throughout the eras of the famous missions and revival movements, the study of the End-Times remained on the back burner of Christian thought. Only recently has eschatology moved more to the forefront of people's minds.

As noted earlier, a quick check of today's Christian bookstore shelves and the staggering sales numbers for fictional and non-fictional depictions of end-time events reveal what is on the minds of those inside and outside the Church. More than ever, believers and unbelievers alike are thinking about the end of the world. A major catalyst for this wave of interest in the End-Times is one of the most prophetic signposts to date: the rebirth of Israel as a nation in 1948 and the return of Jerusalem to Israeli control in 1967. These two events are significant. The destruction of Jerusalem was the main reason those in the early Church stopped believing Jesus would return in their generation. Correspondingly, its rebirth has reestablished a context for Jesus' return and thus has sparked a revival of the study of end-time prophecy. A number of Old Testament prophetic passages would be irrelevant if there were no nation of Israel, no gathering place on Earth for the Jewish people. However, when Israel came back into existence a few decades ago, a context was reestablished for numerous specific and literal end-of-the-age prophecies. These prophecies involve a specific place and a specific people. The City of David, Jerusalem, was chosen as the capital by its ancient namesake because David knew that the location was special to God. God cares deeply about this strategic little plot of land, and has great plans for it. The return of Jews to the land of promise is a major signal to the Church of a change in season. It is the beginning of the sequence of signs and events, which will culminate in the birthing of another age.

So with Israel's rebirth and Jerusalem's return to international prominence, hundreds of chapters of the Bible became relevant again. These passages have been a mystery to many and often completely ignored for almost 2,000 years. Now they can be read and understood with more clarity. For example, when we read about the prediction of blessing for Israel, we can picture a real place on Earth where this will happen. When the writer of a Psalm asks us to pray for Jerusalem and the Jews who live there, we don't have to substitute any other meanings. We can better accept that such passages mean what they say and have considerable relevance to the time in which we live, as well as to the times fast approaching. That is the good news. The downside is that these passages, which we now understand as applying to real places and real people, involve more than promises of victory, blessing and glory. They speak of trouble for Israel and the world unlike anything we can imagine. They involve a storm that will engulf the planet and seriously trouble every man, woman and child. No one will move through the events of the End-Times without much difficulty. Almost no one is prepared for what is to come.

END-TIMES
simplified:

CHAPTER TWO:

How Serious is the Problem?

Jesus listed the signs that will indicate the End-Times are near (Matt. 24:4-8), and called the signs "the beginning of sorrows." The signs themselves will be difficult enough to endure. They will include deceitful and deceptive leaders, wars, ethnic conflicts, famines, plagues, earthquakes, and a significant increase in the persecution of believers. To the generation that witnesses all these signs, they are to be a warning that the events Jesus highlighted as the worst moments in human history are soon to come. These dramatic events will mark the turning point of human history, as mankind embarks on a descent into trouble and judgment. According to Jesus, it will be a time of "great tribulation, such as has not been since the beginning of time, no, nor shall ever be" (Matt. 24:21).

The Bible leaves no room for speculation as to whether other events in world history could have qualified. Historic events involving great death and horror have occurred throughout history and have affected many around the world, but not *everyone* in the world. Regarding the coming events, Jesus said if His Father had not chosen beforehand to cut those days short, no one would survive (Matt. 24:22). The Bible is clear that every single person on the planet will experience the coming trouble. Jesus described "men's hearts failing them from fear and the expectation of those things which are coming on the earth" (Luke 21:26). Paul described a mass exodus of sincere believers from their faith in Jesus (2 Thess. 2:3) due to the horror of those events. The truth is that nobody in Heaven or on Earth has ever seen anything like what the Bible says will happen during the End-Times.

Why will these events be so intense? Why does the coming storm have to be so violent, so massive in scope? The answer is not because God is severe, but because the condition of the Earth will have become so severe that no other course of action would suffice. Sin will be at its height (Dan. 8:23), and darkness and wickedness will be at their worst (Rev. 9:21). Joel described this time as a "day of darkness and gloominess" (Joel 2:2), which is a fair assessment of the eventual fate of God's enemies. It is important to remember that the Book of Revelation, which gives much information about the great trouble that will come, is not about how mad God will be at people, but about how bad mankind will have become, and God's necessary response to that wickedness.

In early September of 2005, eighty percent of New Orleans was under water after being devastated by Hurricane Katrina. The reason some people gave for staying behind when the call went forth to evacuate the city, was that they could not imagine how bad the conditions were going to be. In many ways, it is still unimaginable. Practically overnight, one of the most powerful cities in the world was stripped of its strength. One of the many shocks to people was the transformation of a first-world power into a third-world reality in a day. Many involved in the aftermath said it was the worst thing they had ever seen, and that they were struggling for answers.

A few days later, *Time* magazine mocked the explanation that the hurricane was God's judgment on that city for its sin. The article's author compared that kind of thinking to ancient superstitions that linked natural disasters to angry gods. For a believer, however, there should be no question. Unlike earlier terrorist attacks, when many groped for answers about the source of the trouble, this time the answer is frighteningly easy. We know God controls the natural forces of nature. Can a believer appeal to simple "fate" or some kind of cosmic accident that caught God by surprise? Some of what has taken place over time is the "groan" of creation due to the impact of sin (Rom. 8:19-22). Nothing, however, happens without the knowledge of God, who oversees all of history. We are forced to deal with this fact: according to Jeremiah, God has a controversy with the nations because of sin (Jer. 25:31). We believers are confronted with a God who will, without hesitation, bring judgment to get the attention of His people and the nations of the world, in the hope that they will repent.

We must understand Hurricane Katrina was not a judgment only on New Orleans. It was a judgment on all of us in the western world who embrace any form of darkness, wickedness or compromise. And this hurricane was but a whisper of the Lord; a roar from the Lion will come soon (Amos 3:8). The events of the past few years – terror attacks, tsunamis, hurricanes – are but preludes to the events that will confront us in the End-Times. The problem is not God. And Jesus is unmoved by our definitions of who He is or who we think He should be. He is a King and a Judge who loves us as our Husband. His deep love for all of us motivates Him to declare war on darkness, sin and wickedness. He cannot and will not coexist with His enemies, He will not make peace with them, and He will not ignore them in the name of grace. He is in a war, and His victory prize will be all the people of Earth wholly given to His heart.

Thus, the intensity of what strikes the nations will increase immensely in the years to come. Such events will become more frequent and more severe. These "birth pangs," which Jesus also referred to as the beginning of sorrows, are the beginning of a birthing process. The birthing process will end with the birthing of a new and glorious age, in which the risen and beautiful King Jesus will rule the nations in wisdom, power, majesty and splendor. However, the birthing of this age, an age so gloriously different than the present age, will not happen easily. The birthing process will be painful and difficult. Jesus said in John 16:20-23, "Most assuredly, I say to you that you will weep and lament, but the world will rejoice; and you will be sorrowful, but your sorrow will be turned into joy. A woman, when she is in labor, has sorrow because her hour has come; but as soon as she has given birth to the child, she no longer remembers the anguish, for joy that a human being has been born into the world. Therefore you now have sorrow; but I will see you again and your heart will rejoice, and your joy no one will take from you. And in that day you will ask Me nothing. Most assuredly, I say to you, whatever you ask the Father in My name He will give you."

When we see what has been in the heart of God for us all along, we will forget all the pain and trial we endured before then. We will rejoice after the pain of labor that "a human being has been brought into the world." When the new age has been birthed and we have seen Jesus return, we will be filled with a joy that cannot be taken from us. In that day, we will relate to the Father face to face, and He will give us whatever we ask, whatever our hearts desire. This "asking" in that day will be as the intercession of Jesus in Psalm 2:8: "Ask of Me, and I will give You the nations for Your inheritance, and the ends of the earth for Your possession." The Son relates to the Father through intercession! This is how He loves to relate to the Father. The thing that delights the Son will thrill us as well: approaching the Father in intercession and asking Him for our hearts' desires.

The labor pains before the birth, however, will be intense. There is no romanticism in the heart of a mother about to give birth. She can only prepare herself to endure what is coming. In the same manner, we must not romanticize the End-Times. They will be the darkest days the world has ever seen. Jesus never exaggerates and He used the word "anguish" to describe the kind of trauma *believers* will endure before the birth of the new age. While the world rejoices in its wickedness, believers will weep and mourn, because understanding the nature of the coming storm will make us sorrowful. The birth pangs, these "contractions" that are even now taking place throughout the world, will come with greater frequency and intensity. Eventually, the labor process will move from its early stage to the "breaking of the water" stage, in which a flood of trouble will come, which leads to the heavy labor period. The heavy labor period will in turn lead to the birth of another age.

The early signs Jesus listed are even now unfolding before our eyes. He spoke of false deliverers (messiahs) who would arise in His name and deceive many; false teachers who would use pressure and manipulation to force loyalty and gain a following. He warned that we would hear of wars and rumors of war. In addition to these events, there will be natural catastrophes, such as famines, pestilences, and earthquakes "in various places" (Matt. 24:7). All these events will constitute what Jesus described as "the beginning." They will be the beginning of sorrows; more sorrow will follow. On the heels of these international traumas and natural disasters, there will be a marked increase of persecution and tribulation for believers. Christians will be hated by people in all nations.

Even though all these events, which are just the beginning, may seem unbearable and fearful, Jesus encouraged believers not to be troubled. "The end is not yet," He said, after He spoke of the wars and rumors of war that will grip hearts with fear. Even as nations and ethnic groups rise against each other, and civil disorder, racism, anti-Semitism and economic conflicts and aggression break out, and military and political conflicts flare up, we are not to fear. Matthew 24:6 records Jesus saying, "See that you are not troubled; for all these things must come to pass, but the end is not yet." Jesus meant believers should not be troubled like the rest of the world, because we will have a framework for interpreting these events, which will mystify everyone else. We will understand that God is on the move, orchestrating these events, as things move closer to the end. Even though we will be hated by all nations, we can stand unafraid and secure in God's love for us and His perfect plan.

The Bible explains what will cause all nations to hate all believers.

It is related to the identity and destiny all believers have because of their relationship with Christ. The Bible speaks of "the Bride of Christ" in describing all believers as a group. The Bride of Christ refers to the Church as a whole, the Body of Christ. The Bride is meant to be and will be the equally-yoked companion of Jesus and will intimately partner with Him to rule in justice and righteousness. The Bride of Christ in her fullness will be meek and lowly, simple yet lovely, and possess a passion and power that comes from voluntary weakness and God-given purity. To know Jesus fully, she must first drink from the cup of hardship and suffering and learn self-denial and sacrificial love.

In contrast to the Bride of Christ, Revelation 17:1-7 describes a monstrous figure named "Mystery Babylon," a woman "arrayed in purple and scarlet, and adorned with gold and precious stones and pearls, having in her hands a golden cup full of abominations and the filthiness of her fornication." This "woman" is given the title of "Mystery Babylon" by the Holy Spirit to interpret for us what she represents. She is not a literal woman, but a symbolic representation of a global religion to come that will be mysterious in nature. Her second name, "Babylon," indicates that she represents the world system of human wisdom and not authentic faith birthed from Heaven (James 3:13-18). "Babylonian," or earthly wisdom, is "earthly, sensual, and demonic," James said. "For where envy and self-seeking exist, confusion and every evil thing are there." This mysterious Babylonian religion will appeal, at its core, to the self-seeking and the self-centered nature of mankind.

This woman also represents a corporate people who will be the antithesis of the Bride of Christ. John described this woman, whom he saw in his vision, as a beautiful counterfeit of the Bride, who will entice the wicked nations of the world to choose her and her wickedness over Jesus and His righteousness. Her goal will be to seduce all men into partnering with her to rule the world in wickedness and self-indulgent sin. She is described as being rich and as glorifying herself and living "luxuriously" (Rev. 18:7). Her power will come from her deceptive appeal and alluring lifestyle, promises, and golden cup of sinful pleasures. She will embody the spirit of our current age: self-indulgence, self-gratification and self-worship. She will appeal to the growing universal desire for peace and safety (1 Thess. 5:3), pleasure, comfort and luxury (2 Tim. 3:1-4).

This woman will be extremely alluring. Even John said he marveled at her deceptive beauty when he saw her in his vision (Rev. 17:6-7). She personifies a coming false religious system, which will have economic might behind it and will appeal to people's desire for prosperity and comfort. Economic prosperity will come to those aligned with the false religious system, but the prosperity will be temporary and short-lived. The unifying nature of the system personified by "Mystery Babylon" in Revelation will bring together many different faiths previously in violent conflict with one another. A false sense of peace will come through false unity and agreement among sinful, wicked men. The shallow, surface promises it makes will be ultimately empty; but many will be lured by the hope of peace and safety. Many will believe that what we've all hoped for – world peace – has come at last. They will be perplexed when Christians speak out against the peace and security that has finally been attained.

Christians who are connected to the heart of the Lord in that hour, however, will know what is really going on. They will recognize it as the false "calm" before the coming storm, and will boldly preach truth throughout the nations. They will expose this religious system as a fraud. They will speak against the "scarlet beast" the evil woman of Revelation will be riding as she attempts to maintain her influence (Rev. 17:3). The scarlet beast will be Antichrist himself, though people won't realize it at the time. Christians will expose sin and warn of Jesus' Second Coming. The reality of Jesus dealing with His enemies brutally (Ps. 110:5-6) will upset many, and Christians will be seen as "enemies of the state" and considered threats to the perceived peace. It will be a dark and troubling time for the Church. John described this religious system, this "false bride," as being "drunk with the blood of the saints and with the blood of the martyrs of Jesus" (Rev. 17:6).

The apostle Paul wrote of something else that will happen during this period of time. He called it "the falling away," or the great apostasy, a time when many would become offended at God and leave the Church (2 Thess. 2:3). It will be part of the progression of events about which Jesus spoke in Matthew 24:9, when all the nations will hate Christians. In verses 10-12, Jesus described the unfolding drama of that day: "And then many will be offended, will betray one another, and will hate one another. Then many false prophets will rise up and deceive many. And because lawlessness will abound, the love of many will grow cold." Those in the Church will have to guard against slipping into bitterness and offense towards God. Those who do not know Him intimately will not understand His heart and the reasons for His actions when the trouble comes, and therefore will be offended at Him. They will not like the message their fellow believers preach. There will be betrayal and hatred. People's love will grow cold in an atmosphere of increasing rebellion against God and His ways. Many will leave the Church; and many others will be martyred for their stand.

As all of this unfolds, the final period of mankind's earthly existence will begin, the "breaking of the water" will occur, and the heavy labor period will commence. The heavy labor period is what Jesus called the "Great Tribulation." It will be a time still more intense, more troublesome, than even the trauma of the birth pains. All that has happened up to the time of the Great Tribulation will have been but a mere prelude to the shaking that will next affect the entire world. Revelation 6:8 gives a picture of the early death toll during the final years of trouble, conflict and judgment. One-fourth of the population of the world will die. With Earth's current population, that means 1.5 billion deaths. Based on population growth projections for the next several decades, this number could grow to more than two billion people. This massive death toll defies our imaginations and offends our minds.

The horrific description continues in Revelation 9:15, one of the most chilling verses in the Bible. Many do not know how to deal with it. It says that one-third of what's left of the planet's population will be taken in yet another traumatic event. In today's numbers, that means 1.5 billion more people will die.

This time of great tribulation for the Church will also be the nation of Israel's most difficult hour. In chapter 13 of the book he authored, Zechariah predicted that during the tribulation, two-thirds of the Jewish people would be brutally slaughtered. The prophet Jeremiah called this time of tribulation for the Jews "Jacob's trouble" (Jer. 30:7).

So, combining the numbers described in chapters six and nine of Revelation and chapter 13 of Zechariah, it appears that, according to the Word of God, half the world's population will be swept away in a sudden flood of judgment in the last hours of history. It seems reasonable to many people at this point, to close the Bible and become offended with God; after all, God is identified by John as the One orchestrating these events. Another reasonable response for some is to dismiss these passages, or their interpretations, as hype or the workings of an overdramatic imagination. It is difficult to cope with these passages of the Bible that seem to portray the God we love as cruel, brutal and vicious. The truth is that God is none of these things. He is loving, kind, merciful, beautiful, forgiving, gracious, slow to anger and perfect. It seems so hard to reconcile the truth about God with the disaster that will come, that Christians everywhere simply avoid entire chapters of the Bible they don't understand. The often-asked question is how a loving God could initiate the slaughter of all those men, women and children. Asking this question, however, reveals the extent to which we are uninformed about and unaware of the nature and depth of man's hidden hatred of God and His ways.

God's judgments against stubborn wickedness are because of His goodness and commitment to being in relationship with each of us forever, not because He is angry. Part of the problem is that most people want a God who requires nothing of them, who is easy to figure out and who allows Himself to be under their control. They do not want a King who is inflexible toward rebellion, unmoved by the arguments and whims of people, and incapable of compromise. Thus Earth is not ready to be ruled by Jesus. It must be prepared.

Jesus described this reality by telling a parable to those who thought the Kingdom of God would "appear immediately" (Luke 19:11-27). He told them a story of a nobleman who went to a far country "to receive for himself a kingdom and to return." Jesus was talking about Himself. The nobleman organized his servants and set them about his business. In the meantime, the citizens of the nobleman's kingdom declared their hatred of him, and expressed through their messengers that they would no longer submit to his rule over their lives. After a time, the nobleman returned, settled his accounts with his servants, and dealt with the ones who would not have him as king. In Luke 19:27 He said, "But bring here those enemies of mine, who did not want me to reign over them, and slay them before me."

This terrifying statement was made by the coming King Jesus, who, through the parable, was stating clearly how He would conduct His affairs when He returned. He will deal with His servants first, either rewarding them or punishing them. Then He will deal with His enemies. Both His servants and His enemies face a problem: the King coming back to claim what is His is not who some think He is. For example, the final servant described in the parable did not really know the nobleman, and served Him out of fear. Just as this servant's perception of the master differed from reality, many people's perception of Jesus differs from reality. And just as the servant's misconception affected his choices and lifestyle, so do many people's misconceptions affect how they live. Many today live in a lazy, half-hearted way before God, with the excuse that His commandments are too difficult or don't make sense to them. Ultimately, they will face a much greater difficulty in the coming days.

Do It.

Jesus' enemies, the nations, will not receive Him. They will hate Him then as they hate Him now, though they will have had the opportunity to hear the truth and receive the King. Jesus said that the "gospel of the kingdom will be preached in all the world as a witness to all nations" before the end comes (Matt. 24:14). All the nations will have had a witness, and been given the opportunity to turn from their stubbornness and submit to the coming King before He comes to judge. Despite the opportunity given them, Isaiah 63:1-6 says when the time comes, not one nation will have chosen to stand with Him. He will be forced to slay them all, as they declare war on Him to keep what they feel is theirs (Zech. 12:3; Rev. 16:14; 19:14).

The greatest problem facing humanity, including the Church itself, however, is that almost no one believes these events are real events that will actually occur. Some do not believe in the Jesus of Luke 19:27, Psalm 110:5, and Isaiah 63:6. Even worse, many of the people who do believe these biblical predictions depict real events to come, also believe they will not be on Earth to experience them. Or they believe the end-time passages are relevant, but not for them. They view the passages as being relevant only to unbelievers who ignore God, and reason that the Church has nothing to fear because believers will be long gone when the trouble comes, having left this wicked and sinful world to its fate at the hands of a wrathful God. This perspective of the end-time events to come is tragically erroneous, and will result in many being unprepared for the trials ahead. The Bible is clear that no one will be exempt; no one will emerge unscathed from what is coming. The greatest storm in the history of the world will affect everyone, and almost no one is preparing for it.

END-TIMES
simplified:

CHAPTER THREE:

Who Can Endure It?

The question of the ages is: Who can endure the great and terrible day of the Lord? Preaching to the wicked, corrupt nation of Judah thousands of years ago, the prophet Joel asked them a question: "For the day of the Lord is great and very terrible; who can endure it?" In his vision of the sixth seal judgment, John saw many people crying out, asking a similar question: "For the great day of His wrath has come, and who is able to stand?" (Rev. 6:17). The question is a hard one and we are meant to feel its impact as we read it in Scripture. The question is meant to emphasize the intensity of what Jesus described: a time so severe and traumatic to the world, that we are supposed to wonder if any will be able to bear the weight of it. We are meant to ask what we should do and how we should live so that we can endure it. The questions are meant to burst forth from our hearts and cause a holy fear to arise in us of the God who would ask such a question through His prophet, Joel. We are supposed to tremble at the implications of this question, and to understand that "the fear of the Lord is the beginning of wisdom…" (Prov. 9:10).

In His mercy, God has provided answers for us through Joel.

"Now therefore," says the Lord through His prophetic messenger, "turn to Me with all of your heart, with fasting, with weeping, and with mourning." The Lord has given us the way forward because He is kind and has mercy on us. As human beings, we are ignorant of our true desperate and sinful condition. We are sinful to the core, foolish and short-sighted. We are by nature self-destructive in our behavior. In His kindness, God stops our self-destructive tendencies through judgment, in essence saving us from ourselves, protecting the faithful and righteous, so we can enter into our destiny with Him.

God has warned us that destructive judgment is coming, but has emphasized that there is still time and hope for us. If we will turn away from our part in this judgment, turn to Him with all of our hearts, He will preserve and protect us. That's what He wants to do.

The key to endurance is a whole-hearted turn to God. A whole-hearted turn to God is much more than an initial turning, a momentary turning, or a partial turning. It involves fully turning away *from* one thing and fully turning *to* something else. In Joel's day, Israel turned to all kinds of short-term solutions, rather than to God, to deliver them from trouble. Today, many in the western world turn to all kinds of self-help solutions to make themselves feel better. They build houses on sand, houses not founded on truth or on the rock of the wisdom of Jesus (Matt. 7:24-27). At the end of His great Sermon on the Mount, Jesus gave clear and basic instruction on what a godly lifestyle looks like. Many appreciate the brilliance of this teaching, even as the Jews were "astonished" in the day Jesus taught them; but very few take His words seriously enough to really live this way.

The problem the Church faces is that the coming flood, the Great Tribulation, about which Jesus warned, will be way beyond disruptive. It will be destructive. Only those who do now what Jesus said to do in Matthew 5-7, will remain standing in the midst of it. The ones who remain standing and endure will be the ones described in Revelation 7:9-10. This is the answer to the question of "Who can stand?" posed in Revelation 6:17. It is those who turn whole-heartedly to God and are martyred in the Great Tribulation because of their faith. Later in Revelation, it is said of these people that "they overcame him (Satan) by the blood of the Lamb (Jesus) and the word of their testimony, and they did not love their lives to the death" (Rev. 12:11). How do you survive a flood? Jesus told us in Matthew 7:24-27 that the way we survive a flood is by building our houses on solid foundations, which means living godly lifestyles of obedience, prayer and fasting.

The ones who stand will have, by the time of the tribulation, fully turned from the ways of this world. They will have fully turned from a self-indulgent and self-gratifying culture, and therefore will not be fooled by the false promises of the counterfeit bride. They will have no interest in personal glory and have no illusions about the futility of worldly gain. This life will hold no allure for them. They will have built their lives on the rock of truth, and will hold tightly to what is real, even if it results in death. Death will have no sting for them. In that day, during the trouble that comes, they may die, but they will taste sweet victory before the throne of the Lamb. Then they will enjoy their great reward when Jesus returns to Earth. There is great promise, reward and blessing (Joel 2:14) for those who fully turn to God with all of their hearts.

Turning to God with all our hearts means making a sincere commitment to reach for God with all of our might. There may be times when we fall short, but we will not be denied by God. We must keep reaching, even after failure. We must allow His great love to spur us on. After we commit to turn to God with all our hearts, we need direction about how to do so, about how to walk out our commitment.

This brings us back to Jesus' Sermon on the Mount. In this sermon, He described the lifestyle we are to live. Living the way Jesus told us to live is the way we turn, the way we walk out our commitment. We are meant to rend our hearts and not our garments

(Joel 2:13). To "rend the heart" means to pay the internal or emotional cost of really turning to Jesus and doing things His way. An outward pretense of contrition does not matter to Him. Spiritual or high-sounding language is insufficient. Only true internal change will accomplish anything. Matthew 5:3-4 records what Jesus said about the blessings of being "poor in spirit" and of "mourning." A person who is poor in spirit or who is mourning, has grasped the gravity of a situation. They know they are in a crisis, and they know they have no resources within themselves to bring relief. They know there are no earthly solutions to their problems, and no self-help book can save them. No positive message can be uplifting enough. They have come to the place of true barrenness and they recognize they are in a state of true spiritual poverty. Coming to this place of "spiritual barrenness," is the best gift from God any of us can receive, because we won't allow God to rescue us until we realize we need to be rescued.

The Israelites did not understand the depth of their problem after the locust plagues came and completely devoured their crops. They thought the problem was a lack of natural resources, food, drink and fuel for their lamps that occurred because of the locust devastation. They had no idea that God's judgment was their real problem. Their prideful and complete disregard for God, their compromise, and their embrace of darkness, had set them on a collision course with God's judgment. They had no way to save themselves from the storm of judgment that eventually came.

The current plight of the nations of the world, particularly the western world, is the same as Israel's. In the case of America, some people think the problem we face is economic. Some think it is a lack of education, and others think it's a poorly trained and equipped military. None of these is even close. The real problem is that, as a whole, Americans are living a lie. Most Americans believe the country to be a "spiritual" nation with a Christian foundation, but there are few people living the godly or righteous lifestyle described by Jesus in the Sermon on the Mount. There is almost no righteousness or passion for God in the political sphere or the marketplace. There also is very little in the Church. Only when Americans recognize and acknowledge our lack of passion and authentic righteousness, will we have any hope of finding the true solution: turning to God. Our wickedness makes us enemies of God. Our only hope is to truly "rend our hearts," not put on an outward show of contrition or humility with no basis in reality.

Recognizing our spiritual poverty is a true gift from God that is available to anyone who wants to receive it. Those who receive this gift will enter also into the blessing that comes from mourning (Matt. 5:4). True mourning is birthed by God in the hearts of those who turn to Him. Those who mourn see clearly the true condition of things and yearn deeply for change. The person who sees the smallness of what *is* compared to the greatness of what *could be*, according to the Word of God, truly mourns with passion for change. The possibilities in God are glorious, and those who mourn are blessed because they will eventually be comforted when the possibilities become realities. What they desire – to be satisfied by God alone – will come to them in time. In the meantime, however, there will be much pain and struggling. The pain must be willingly embraced by all who desire the breakthrough of supernatural power from God called "grace." God's grace brings true life and spiritual wealth internally, both now and in the age to come. The pain of the delay and the lack of internal reality produce meekness and humility (Matt. 5:5), which Jesus is working to ultimately produce in us. Jesus said when we have meekness, we will "inherit the earth" (Matt. 5:5). He was not speaking metaphorically. Those who are meek will literally inherit the Earth.

Jesus' solution for the coming crisis seems unusual to our strength-focused minds. He wants us to voluntarily embrace weakness. The wisest thing we can do is recognize our true condition, which produces mourning. Mourning in turn produces humility, the realization that there is a more excellent way than our own. If we embrace Jesus' anointed pattern for living, and fully agree to live His way – praying, fasting, obeying and studying the Word of God with intensity – we will begin to think like Him and evaluate things based on His value system. Embracing the life of a servant cultivates a "hunger and thirst for righteousness" (Matt. 5:6), and we become fully committed to His plan. Those who live Jesus' way will endure the coming trial and stand. Equally important, they will be trained in the process to rule with Him.

To rule with Jesus, we must learn how to rule like Jesus. God delights in mercy, so we must begin to delight in mercy. When we realize how mercifully God deals with us despite our weakness, we become more tender and kind to others who are weak. When we grasp how much God loves us, we begin to love others better. When we comprehend the depths of God's kindness, it becomes rooted in us and we are more kind.

God is "gracious and merciful, slow to anger, and of great kindness" (Joel 2:13), and will gladly receive those who turn or return to Him. This offers hope and assurance to those who truly want to turn to Him and reject sin and wickedness. God's kindness is not intended to give us license to continue in sin. His mercy and graciousness are intended to give us courage to break our ties with darkness and turn to Him with all of our hearts. Better still, as we fully turn to Him, He will turn toward us (Joel 2:14). When God turns toward a people, the result is the outpouring of revival and the release of power. It is possible for God to relent from His judgment to a measure, if people turn to Him, and He may even leave a blessing behind in the process (Joel 2:14).

God is calling the Church to pray and contend for a widespread turning of hearts. The Lord is summoning an entire generation of young adults to gather in what Joel called a "sacred assembly" or a solemn assembly (Joel 2:15). Gathering in this manner is what the Bible instructs us to do when facing a time of trouble. God's solution is for His people to gather and hold prayer meetings. Every time Jesus spoke about the End-Times, He included a mandate to prayer (Matt. 24:13; Mark 13:33-37; Luke 21:34-36). Prayer is the solution Isaiah gave to the king of Israel in Isaiah 8:16-18. The king of Judah was facing a crisis. Armies from the north were coming to invade his nation and remove him from power. His nation was caught in a power struggle between the super-powers of that time. He weighed his political options, trying to figure out which nations had the military strength to help him escape this dilemma. Isaiah told the king to forget about these untrustworthy nations and run to God. And he encouraged the king to rally the people to pray. Imagine having to tell the President of the United States that his only hope against a major military enemy is to hold prayer meetings!

Those who turn fully to God, gather in prayer, and ask for mercy, take on God's burden for the sin and wickedness of the nation. Mourning and weeping come forth in our hearts and spirits from this place of prayer. A unity with God comes with the turning of our hearts, as we join our hearts to His and care about what He cares about. When He finds people loyal to Him, He will "show Himself strong on their behalf" (2 Chr. 16:9). God shows Himself strong by turning and relenting, and possibly leaving a blessing behind. The eyes of the Lord are scouring the Earth, searching for the ones who will turn away from darkness and turn to Him so that He might show Himself strong. Regarding His Second Coming, Jesus Himself asked, "Nevertheless, when the Son of Man comes, will He really find faith on the earth?" (Luke 18:8). Jesus was asking if He would find anyone who "believes that He is, and that He is a rewarder of those who diligently seek Him" (Heb. 11:6).

Though great trouble will come to the Church and to the nations, it is not God's desire that any should perish. He does not want to lose a single soul to the fires of Hell. Paul said God "desires all men to be saved and to come to the knowledge of the truth" (1 Tim. 2:4). Peter said God is "not willing that any should perish but that all should come to repentance" (2 Pet. 3:9). Peter was not speaking about unbelievers. He was speaking about believers in the Church, and God's desire that none of them would perish in the great falling away from the faith that will come. The issue of who in the Church can endure the coming trial was heavy on Peter's heart as he wrote this letter to the Body of Christ.

The first thing Peter wanted Christians to understand is that in the End-Times scoffers will come and will contribute to the falling away of some in the Church. They will scoff at the promise of the return of Jesus, and will be the worst enemies of those serious about preparing for the End-Times. For those of us determined to live the kind of lifestyles that will equip us to stand, accusation and scoffing will come from the most unexpected people, even friends and loved ones. According to Peter, the reason they will accuse and scoff is because they will "walk according to their own lusts" (2 Pet. 3:3). They will have a different agenda for their lives than the one Jesus has. The message of His coming will be disruptive and uncomfortable for them, because they would need to make big changes and shift all their priorities if the message were true. For people committed to their own agendas and lifestyles, this message will provoke anger, and they will express their anger by scoffing at and mocking the message and the messengers. Peter wrote of such scoffing and reactionary words: "Where is the promise of His coming? For since the fathers fell asleep, all things continue as they were from the beginning of creation" (2 Pet. 3:4). Because of their self-centered agendas and their anger at a message that would disturb their lives, they will then "willfully forget" the nature of God and His divine timetable.

Despite their scoffing and mocking, God still will love the scoffers. He loves everyone because He has created them. Peter explained that Jesus' delay in coming will be because of His mercy. He will not forget His promise, for His name is Faithful and True (Rev. 19:11). He delights in keeping His word and following through on His commitment to us. However, He does not desire anyone to perish. He will delay His return as long as He can to make a way for as many as possible to come into repentance and turn to Him with their whole hearts.

As scoffers come against us, we must guard against falling away. God has told us beforehand what will come so we can prepare. "Beware lest you also fall from your own steadfastness, being led away with the error of the wicked; but grow in the grace and knowledge of our Lord and Savior Jesus Christ" (2 Pet. 3:17-18). Some in the Church have fallen away already. Many, many more will not endure the coming times. To endure, we must hold fast to truth and be determined to grow in grace and knowledge of Jesus. Paul prayed in Ephesians 1:17 that we would receive from God the "spirit of wisdom and revelation in the knowledge of Him." Our only hope of standing until the end is to break away from the deception of sin and the error of wickedness. We must give ourselves to lives of praying, fasting, and growing in the knowledge of who Jesus is and what He is like. Only that will save us from becoming offended in the coming days.

In Luke 21:34-36, Jesus said, "But take heed to yourselves, lest your hearts be weighed down with carousing, drunkenness, and cares of this life, and that Day come on you unexpectedly. For it will come as a snare on all those who dwell on the face of the whole earth. Watch therefore, and pray always that you may be counted worthy to escape all these things that will come to pass, and to stand before the Son of Man."

If we want to stand, to endure what is coming, we must "take heed to ourselves." We must examine our hearts to determine if we are weighed down by distraction, self-indulgence, worry or fear. We must receive from God an accurate picture of our spiritual condition. The only answer is to pay attention to what is going on around us and view it from God's perspective. Once we see from His perspective and understand that the Great Tribulation is coming and why, we must pray.

We must gather in worship and prayer, humbling ourselves before Him and turning from any and all sin in our lives. If we do this, He promises to hear our prayer from Heaven, forgive our sin, and heal our land (2 Chr. 7:14). This is the way in which He "counts us worthy" and the only way to partner with God in His desire for mercy. His heart is to show the nations mercy, not bring judgment.

He is searching, however, for those on Earth who will agree with Him in intercession. Intercession is the only thing that will cause Him to decrease the severity of what is coming. It is the only thing that will cause Him to open up pockets of mercy over regions and cities in the midst of judgment. Part of God's glorious plan for the Church is to draw her into His plan to bring great revival to the land, both before and in the midst of unprecedented judgment.

ENDTIMES
simplified:

CHAPTER FOUR:

God's Great Plan for the Church

Having a basic understanding of God's goals and what He will accomplish helps us understand eschatology. Understanding His objectives is vital to grasping why His judgments will be so intense. God's objective has to do with Jesus' relationship with the Church, the Bride of Christ. The Father's desire has always been to present His Son with a Bride, which He will do at the end of the age. The Church's story in this present age will end with the most glorious wedding ever. Ephesians 5:25-27 gives a picture of who we are to Jesus and what it is for which He is diligently working. "Husbands, love your wives, just as Christ also loved the church and gave Himself for her, that He might sanctify and cleanse her with the washing of water by the word, that He might present her to Himself a glorious church, not having spot or wrinkle or any such thing, but that she should be holy and without blemish."

Everything God is doing and will do has to do with His desire to present the Church to His Son Jesus as a pure, spotless Bride. Jesus, for His part, is working diligently to sanctify and cleanse His Bride through God's Word, which, when internalized, changes our desires, emotions and thoughts. When our minds are filled with

Scripture, we think and feel differently. The Holy Spirit, the Spirit of Truth, partners with Jesus to cause our hearts and minds to come alive in a new way when heavenly truths take root. Jesus will have a Bride equally yoked to Him. To be equally yoked with Jesus, we must be transformed to think and feel as Jesus does. Paul spoke of this in 2 Corinthians 6:14: "Do not be unequally yoked with unbelievers. For what fellowship has righteousness with lawlessness? And what communion has light with darkness?"

Many people understand that Jesus desires a pure, spotless Bride, but they don't know why. Intimate partnership with mankind is the highest delight of the Father, Son and Holy Spirit. The awesome news of the Gospel goes far beyond forgiveness of our sins. The glorious and unbelievable destiny of all believers is to have intimacy with God, to partner with Jesus as His Bride, and to gain access to the deepest places of God's heart.

Being equally yoked means bearing a burden together, like two oxen in a yoke, helping one another carry the weight by sharing the burden equally. The idea is not that we will be as Jesus, but that we will be like-minded and like-hearted as we go with Him where He goes. As an equally-yoked partner, we will bring in the fullness of joy by being like-minded (Phil. 2:1-4), "having the same love, being of one accord, of one mind."

Sharing Jesus' burdens as we share His heart and His thoughts is what makes us an equally-yoked partner for Him. The concept of being Jesus' equally-yoked Bride goes much deeper than the earthly example of a believer marrying another believer. The idea is that true intimacy develops when those who love one another share the deepest places of their hearts with each other, and are like-minded in their values, desires and priorities. Passion runs deep when the same amount of love given is received. In the earthly example, if one party is madly in love with Jesus and passionately pursuing Him, but her companion is lukewarm, there will be a fundamental discrepancy in how they each live life before God. Seeds of discord will be sown in their relationship and it will lack intimacy.

The journey of becoming equally-yoked lovers of Jesus moves us from a place of fundamental disagreement with His leadership to a place of profound agreement and affection as we submit to His leadership in our lives. The Father's desire has always been to orchestrate the events of history to produce a Bride worthy of Jesus, who is full of all glory and honor and praise. All the pressures of history, combined with the greatest pressure still to come, will produce a people, a Bride, worthy of the One to whom they will be given and the glorious inheritance they will receive as a result.

Daniel 7:27 describes the inheritance we will receive: "Then the kingdom and dominion, and the greatness of the kingdoms under the whole heaven, shall be given to the people, the saints of the Most High. His kingdom is an everlasting kingdom, and all dominions shall serve and obey Him." Daniel had seen a troubling vision of the saints being overcome by a powerful enemy. Daniel said the vision left him "grieved in my spirit within my body, and the visions of my head troubled me" (Dan. 7:15). He asked an angel standing by whether what he had seen was true, and the angel gave him the interpretation of the vision, which had to do with the great and powerful enemy who will make war against the saints and prevail against them (Dan. 7:21). This formidable enemy who will arise in the days ahead is known to us as the Antichrist. The glorious part of the interpretation was, though this man prevailed against the saints for a season, the Ancient of Days came "and a judgment was made in favor of the saints of the Most High, and the time came for the saints to possess the kingdom" (Dan. 7:22). The good news in which we can be confident is, though we will suffer, the story will dramatically shift in our favor at the critical hour, and we will have victory. All the kingdom, dominion, and greatness will be given to us as the Bride of Jesus Christ, the One who will come to Earth to rule all "peoples, nations, and languages" (Dan. 7:14).

Paul wrote, "Do you not know that the saints will judge the world? And if the world will be judged by you, are you unworthy to judge the smallest matters? Do you not know that we shall judge angels?

How much more, things that pertain to this life?" (1 Cor. 6:2-3). He shared this information with the Corinthians because they were going before unbelieving judges to settle disputes and lawsuits. Paul appealed to them by contrasting their current practices with that for which Jesus would prepare them and all other believers: judging the nations with wisdom and righteousness. Our God-given authority will not come automatically or easily, but will be accomplished in our natural maturing process under the leadership of Jesus. As we grow in the knowledge of Him, we will be prepared to rule with Him. As we become like Him in our thoughts, emotions and value systems, we will become able to rule like Him.

The angel in Daniel 11:35 said, "And some of those with understanding (prophetic messengers instructing the Church in the End-Times) shall fall, to refine them, purify them, and make them white, until the time of the end…" The trouble coming to the nations will come in part because of Jesus' strategy to take a lukewarm, compromising, half-hearted, double-minded Church and refine and purify her until she is equally yoked, fully given to His leadership and ways, and mature in her knowledge of Jesus and His heart. He will purify us and we will come to trust Him completely, and be fully confident in Him, even during the severity and trauma of the End-Times.

According to Paul, there are two ways to lay hold of the knowledge of Jesus and become like Him. The first is by entering into the "fellowship of suffering" and the second is by experiencing the "power of His resurrection" (Phil. 3:10). Some believers want the power of His resurrection without sharing in the suffering of the cross. However, Jesus knows that the best way for us to experience the deepest love and rise to the highest level of obedience, is for us to experience shaking, discomfort, and struggles, and learn how to successfully overcome obstacles. He knows the ones who love the most intensely will fight the hardest to win, so He has ordered our lives accordingly.

Beauty Preparations

With Jesus as the leader of our lives, we enter into the knowledge of Him through the power of His resurrection and the fellowship of His sufferings, being conformed to His death (Phil. 3:10). Through the manifestation of His glory and power in our lives, as well as the fire of tribulation, we are perfected into His likeness. It will be through an unprecedented outpouring in both dimensions that what can be called the "beauty preparations of the Bride" will be completed. Esther 2:9-12 gives a picture of what "beauty preparations" for a bride looked like. Beauty preparations in Esther's day called for a six-month treatment of oil of myrrh, the burial spice, which represented death; and a six-month treatment of fragrant perfumes that pleased the senses and transformed the atmosphere of a room. The Book of Esther says that when her beauty preparations were finished, Esther went to see the king and learn if He would delight in her and call her by name (Esth. 2:14). When Esther was presented to him, the king loved her more than all other women, set a crown upon her head, and gave her favor and grace in his sight more than any other (Esth. 2:17).

The story of Esther is a prophetic picture of the beauty preparations that the Church, the Bride of Christ, will experience. These preparations will reach their maximum intensity at the end of the age. The Great Tribulation (the oil of myrrh) will come in the midst of the unparalleled manifestation of God's glory and power (the fragrant perfumes). Though the tribulation will be worse than ever, the Church will walk in greater works than the ones Jesus performed (John 14:12). The meek and humble Bride will be unified with Jesus. Even now, the Bride is being prepared to operate in unprecedented power, in concert with the Holy Spirit. The prepared Bride will partner with Jesus to loose judgment on the nations of the world, and will rule in authority with Him for 1,000 years. Psalm 149 says, "He beautifies the humble with salvation," and in their glory they are joyful, as their praise becomes a weapon of judgment, vengeance and punishment in the hands of God to humble the arrogant nations.

Only God can orchestrate the events of history to produce a Bride worthy and capable of walking in such a high level of anointing and authority, and to prepare His people to judge angels and the people of Earth. Jesus' Bride will be fully mature in love. She will burn with the love of the Father alive in her. This was the prayer of Jesus recorded in John 17:26. He prayed that the same love the Father has for Him would be in us as well. Some assume God will answer this prayer by "snapping His fingers" and making us in an instant fully mature and fully in love with Jesus. Some assume this life and this age are about choosing which team we want to join, based on our definition of salvation. After we pick teams, those who have chosen God will at some point be made obedient and wise automatically.

However, God has a bigger plan and a more effective process to which He is fully committed. This life is about so much more than picking teams. It is about the journey God desires and requires each believer to make to know Him completely. It is a journey of the heart. Our hearts start out cold and become warmer and warmer, until they are on fire with love for God, and whole-heartedly in love with Jesus. God never forces anyone to take the journey. It is a voluntary journey that produces a voluntary, pure, unreserved love for Jesus. The depth to which we fall in love with God will be proportionate to the amount of time and energy we spend learning about and giving ourselves to the journey He has ordained for each of us. Love is not automatic, and neither is intimacy. How much more so a relationship with a transcendent God!

It is impossible to love God whole-heartedly without help, but He helps us. Through the fire of tribulation and the journey of preparation, God lovingly stabilizes our minds, hearts, emotions and wills. When we fully understand His perfect plans, our love for Him will be intense, fiery and eternal. We will continually cry, "Great and marvelous are your works! Oh! The depth of the riches both of the wisdom and the knowledge of God!" (Rev. 15:3; Rom. 11:33).

The Church will emerge from the fire of trouble and hardship as a fully mature and stable Bride, totally dependent on Jesus and trusting Him completely (Song 8:5; Hag. 2:7; Heb. 12:26).

Walking through the fire of tribulation will also produce tenderness and humility in those who refuse to be offended by God's leadership. In addition to changing the way we love God, the fire will change the way we love and relate to one another. Jesus desires for us to love one another in a drastically different manner than we usually do. He said, "This is my commandment, that you love one another as I have loved you" (John 15:12). Sacrificial love flows out of a heart tenderized by the divine process, and is the highest form of love. It can only come from someone who has experienced death to self, self-preservation and selfish ambition. God works in us to develop love that is *holy*, not just pure, and utterly different than any other kind of love we've known. John called this kind of love "perfected love" (1 John 4:17), love that only comes from abiding in Jesus.

Paul too spoke about this love. In his first letter to the Corinthians, he wrote, "But when that which is perfect has come, then that which is in part will be done away..." (verse 13:10); and, "For now we see in a mirror dimly, but then face to face. Now I know in part, but then I shall know just as I am known" (verse 13:12). Often people interpret these two verses to mean we will receive a download of divine information. They imagine an exciting day when perfect knowledge will come and they will know all things. These verses do not refer to our receiving information. They are right in the middle of the love chapter. They are about relationships. When love is perfected in us, we will relate to one another like Jesus relates to us, with holy and pure love. We'll have no ambition, envy or pride; nor will we compare ourselves with others. Those who currently struggle to relate to others will be enabled to develop true relationships and know others intimately. Our love will be sincere and meaningful because our love and the love of others will have been perfected.

Love is perfected as we walk through difficulty and pain. We gain godly perspective and learn true meekness, which allow us to value one another and relate to one another as Jesus values and relates to us. Possessing perfected love means having the capacity to know and be known deeply in our relationships with God and one another. Ultimately, we will approach relationships with tenderness and we will sincerely love mercy, do justly, and walk humbly (Mic. 6:8). We will love and serve sacrificially and selflessly, and put the interests of others above our own for the sake of love. It is crucial that we learn to walk in this kind of love as part of our training and preparation to lead the nations with Jesus.

Salvation to the Uttermost

The glorious destiny of all believers is to be with God for eternity. Unfortunately, many people live mostly for today. They live in fear before God and man because they feel they have much to lose by submitting to God's leadership. They are content to hope God's eternal destiny for them will somehow work itself out later. This is not God's desire for any of us, and Jesus is completely committed to His Father's plan to produce a pure and spotless Bride. God's plan for the Church is far better than we can imagine, and far better than what most people labor for in their daily lives. God's plan involves more than just our initial salvation. It involves our being "saved to the uttermost." The author of Hebrews wrote, "Therefore He is also able to save to the uttermost those who come to God through Him, since He always lives to make intercession for them" (verse 7:25).

Jesus lives to make intercession for all believers. When we come to His Father through Him, He fights for us night and day. He prays to the Father continually for us, that we would be "saved to the uttermost." Jesus contends for much more in our lives than only our initial salvation from Hell. Our prayer to accept Jesus Christ and receive salvation is but the beginning of our journey to uttermost salvation. Salvation in its fullest sense means to be delivered into safety. When David appealed to the "God of his salvation," uttermost salvation was on his mind. He was thankful to God, who delivered him from all his enemies.

Jesus is a safe Savior. Though loving Him can seem risky and does involve intense trials, He is still our safest choice. We don't always believe this. We often speak in bold but empty phrases and clichés about victory, but are unwilling to risk moving out of our comfort zones or releasing our false notions of safety to go where He leads us. Our places of comfort thus become our prisons. Believers gripped by hidden or deep-rooted fear find it difficult to encounter Jesus as He truly is: Savior, Bridegroom, King *and* Judge. They find it easier to explain away the violent passages of the Bible, the judgment passages, than to wrestle with the idea of a God who will bring severe judgment.

Jesus' passion to have an intimate relationship with us now, flows out of His knowledge of our destiny in the age to come. As we continually inquire of the Lord and wonder what lies ahead for our lives in this age, we must remember that everything we do in this age is laying the foundation for what will happen in the next. The early Church's apostolic leadership urged believers to stand fast and endure trials and the fire of testing in light of what lay beyond this life. Their message was a timeless one and applies to us as well. Peter called it our "living hope" and "the end of your faith" (1 Pet. 1:3-9), which was "the salvation of your souls." Salvation to the uttermost means complete deliverance from a world under the dominion of a demonic system. This demonic system is the enemy of western culture, and promotes a gospel of self-indulgence and fleshly delights. John warned in 1 John 2:15-17 not to "love the world or the things in the world…" for "the world is passing away, and the lust of it; but he who does the will of God abides forever."

The world and all its external enemies don't compare to the most treacherous enemy of all: our own wicked and deceitful hearts (Jer. 17:9). Salvation to the uttermost involves being healed from our brokenness and our false and soulish mindsets, which affect the way we live before and relate to God. Jeremiah cried out for such a healing work of God to take place, no matter how painful the process would be (Jer. 17:14). He endured persecution and pressure from his countrymen because of his preaching (17:18), but he chose to submit to God's leadership, as painful and costly as he knew it might be. Jeremiah's submission to God's leadership meant he had to accept what the Lord said He would do: "I, the LORD, search the heart; I test the mind, even to give every man according to his ways, according to the fruit of his doings" (Jer 17:10).

The maturing process through which God takes us is often painful and hard. Those living on Earth when Jesus returns will undergo the most painful and difficult testing of any generation. Only possessing the kind of faith that pleases God will enable them to stay steady, unshakable and unmoved by the fire of testing. The kind of faith that pleases God, according to the writer of Hebrews, involves two things. First, we must believe in the existence of God; and second, we must believe in the true nature of God. The writer of Hebrews says, "…for he who comes to God must believe that He is and that He is a rewarder of those who diligently seek Him" (verse 11:6).

Believing in both the existence and the true nature of God, that He is a rewarder, empowers us to press on in the midst of obstacles and testing. If we believe that He *is*, that He exists, we will be forced to reconcile with Him. Reconciling with Him will lead us to discover that He is a *rewarder*. For those who diligently seek Him; for those who come to the Father through the Son; for those who stand fast with endurance; and for those who rejoice even in the midst of trial and testing and do not draw back; there will be a *great* reward (Heb. 10:35-38). Peter said our inheritance will be "…an inheritance incorruptible and undefiled and that does not fade away, reserved in heaven for you, who are kept by the power of God through faith for salvation ready to be revealed in the last time" (1 Pet. 1:4-5).

We must believe God is a rewarder and desires to "keep us for salvation" by giving us supernatural understanding of who He is. If we believe He is good and will reward us if we seek Him and do not draw back, our faith will have great reward indeed. Peter explained: "In this you greatly rejoice though now for a little while, if need be, you have been grieved by various trials, that the genuineness of your faith, being more precious than gold that perishes, though it is tested by fire, may be found to praise, honor, and glory at the revelation (return to the Earth) of Jesus Christ" (1 Pet. 1:6-7). When we are grieved by various trials, but trust God despite our grief, renewal is produced in our hearts, and we are prepared for eternal glory (2 Cor. 4:16-5:8). Afflictions work for us, not against us, according to Paul, in that they prepare us to receive our rewards (2 Cor. 4:17). Through affliction, God builds a faith in us that will enable us to stand the coming tests and trials. Even in the darkest of hours, we must not lose heart. The God who will orchestrate the most intense and troubling time in history, is the same God who is working and will continue to work for us. Our faith will not be genuine until we've endured these "momentary, light afflictions" (2 Cor. 4:17). They last for but a moment; whereas our reward from God will be everlasting. As we keep our eyes on our future reward, we will be empowered to stand steady in obedience and tenderness, even while many are swept away by the troubles of the End-Times.

The Eternal Destiny of the Saints

In describing his vision, Daniel said, "...the Ancient of Days came, and a judgment was made in favor of the saints of the Most High, and the time came for the saints to possess the kingdom" (Dan. 7:22). He was not referring to some distant, heavenly reality. The Kingdom of which Daniel spoke was Earth and its nations and peoples. The Father Himself has said, "He who overcomes will inherit all things, and I will be his God and he will be My son" (Rev. 21:7). Together with Jesus, we will be entrusted with the utmost responsibility: walking in unprecedented power and authority, yet remaining free of any corruption. It will be the first time humans will possess this much power and not be swayed or corrupted by it.

Throughout history people have demonstrated that when they possess power, they often become self-serving, greedy and bankrupt. In our deception and arrogance, we have used power to elevate our own needs, forsaking mercy and compassion, and ignoring the poor, needy and helpless. When He returns, Jesus will demonstrate what righteous leadership looks like. He will lead the people of Earth in perfection and righteousness, and the saints will be right there beside Him.

This coming Kingdom will be established as Jesus and the saints of the Most High labor together to rebuild, restore and renew the "broken places" (Is. 61:4-7). We will partner with Jesus to redeem and heal the land (2 Chr. 7:13-14); and bring it into the fullness of God's original design prior to the fall of mankind (Rom. 8:18-25). God's original, never-forgotten mandate to mankind will be fulfilled: to fill the Earth with His glory and subdue it (Gen. 1:28; Is. 6:3; Hab. 2:14). Jesus and His Bride also will fulfill the Great Commission of discipling all the nations of Earth (Matt. 28:18-20), and teaching them to observe all that He commands. While God is pleased with the Church's efforts throughout history to disciple all the nations, only Jesus will be able to complete the Great Commission before presenting the Kingdom back to His Father (1 Cor. 15:24). Jesus will disciple and train every sector of society to follow His anointed pattern of living given in the Sermon on the Mount. Even our ruling the Earth with Jesus will be only the beginning of the beginning of our eternal journey with Him. What comes after that is beyond our imagination. Truly, "Eye has not seen, nor ear heard, nor have entered into the heart of man the things which God has prepared for those who love Him" (1 Cor. 2:9).

ENDTIMES
simplified:

CHAPTER FIVE:

God's Great Plan for the Nations

No tactician or strategist can match the brilliance of God. God's amazing end-time plan will fulfill every biblical prophetic promise and decree through the actions of believers and unbelievers. The remarkable part is that when God's plan for this age has come to fruition, He will have perfectly orchestrated thousands of years of history without ever once violating anyone's free will. God allows wicked sinners who hate Him and curse His name to choose their way, and He enables tender-hearted lovers of Him to grow in love. Both groups are allowed to make their choices freely, and still God will have His way. Nothing surprises God. Every person's choices, for good or for evil, contribute to the fulfillment of His plan. Even in the darkest moments of history, people will follow God's prophetic script perfectly, though He will never violate our God-given freedom to make our own choices.

We must trust that God's plan will unfold exactly as He desires it to unfold, and we must accept that God will be totally in control of all the events that will come. Nothing escapes God's eye, and He will never be thwarted by people's best attempts to overthrow Him and replace His leadership with their own. God will continue moving forward with His plan, and whether we like it or not, all of us are participating and will participate in it.

When Israel became a nation again more than fifty years ago, it was secular-minded men who made that decision. All of them chose to vote as they did for reasons of their own. It was one of the most significant prophetic events in history and a key part of God's plan for Israel. God's sovereign plan was accomplished through the free-will actions of carnal-minded, self-serving leaders. The same was true of Jesus' crucifixion. Though wicked men, acting of their own accord, executed the Savior of the world, it all happened exactly as God had planned for it to happen. The same dynamic is happening in our day. As in the cases of Israel's reestablishment as a nation and Christ's crucifixion, God's sovereign plan for the end of the age will happen just as it was always meant to.

Psalm 2 is one of the key end-time passages in the Bible. It helps us understand that God sees what the leaders of nations are planning even now in the secret places of their hearts. It also shows us how God's own plan will unfold. Again, sinful and wicked people will make their plans, but God in His mercy will invite them to rethink those plans. He will give them every opportunity to turn away from their fruitless schemes and embrace His plan. Ultimately, when some freely choose to refuse His invitation, even their refusal will be an essential part of God's plan.

In the context of the End-Times, we must understand that the men about whom Psalm 2 speaks will not be so bound by destiny and the plans of God that they have no free will. While their actions and choices will be known to God, these men will not be forced to choose as they will. Nothing is so predestined that fate and God's will are the only things steering the course of history. In His sovereignty, God has indeed determined the primary events in His eternal plan. He will surely accomplish what He has determined, regardless of what people or demons do. However, He also has chosen to give us a dynamic role in determining to some measure the quality of life we will experience in both the natural and the spiritual realms, now and in the age to come.

The choices we make indicate how responsive we are to God's

grace and how intimately we are in relationship with Him. The depth of our prayer life and the level of our meekness influence our choices. God opens doors of blessing and closes doors of oppression in response to our prayers. There are blessings God has determined to give, but He'll only give them if His people rise up in prayer and ask for them. In keeping with His Father's nature and character, Jesus will continue to rule the world this way after His Second Coming.

Some confuse God's foreknowledge with predestination. They embrace a doctrine of inevitability and relinquish their ordained partnership with God. God has indeed set the primary events of the future, such as the promised ultimate victory of Jesus. And God does reveal many aspects of the future because He already knows what will happen. This does not mean, however, that we have no choices to make in our lives. Consider the example of how a human father understands his young children. He knows with a certain amount of accuracy what his children will choose to do if left alone. He could write a checklist and a time line of what choices they will make and when, and then explain their thought process behind each choice. The father's foreknowledge, however, does not mean his children are bound to his predictions, even if every prediction were to come true. The children could still choose to cooperate, share, get along and clean up after themselves. He knows, however, that they most likely will not make such choices because of their lack of maturity. God knows us thousands of times better than a parent knows his own children and He knows exactly where history is headed; but this does not mean every aspect of the future is predetermined and unchangeable.

In His desire for us to participate in shaping history, God has given us the gift of prayer. God leaves some aspects of the future related to quality of life surprisingly open-ended, and says in His Word that we can make an impact on the future by praying and interceding, whether alone or corporately. This stunning truth is communicated throughout Scripture. For example, James 4:2 says, "you have not because you ask not." In Ezekiel 22:30 the Lord said He was searching for a man among the Israelites who would "stand in the gap" by interceding and praying for Israel, "that I might not destroy it; but I found no one." 2 Chronicles 7:14 says, "If my people, who are called by my name will humble themselves and seek My face, and turn from their wicked ways, then I will hear from heaven, and will forgive their sin and heal their land." Both Joel 2:12-14 and Zephaniah 2:1-3 also leave an open-ended possibility before the people of God regarding their future if they choose to gather and pray with repentance and meekness.

People who fervently believe prayer changes things become the most dedicated intercessors. By praying and interceding, we partner with God in His governance and leadership. Partnering with God through prayer gives dignity to our lives and labors, and greater meaning to our relationship with Him. God does not want us to settle for a one-sided relationship, in which we expect an all-powerful God to call all the shots and condescendingly allow us to come along for the ride. In a way, God does condescend to us, but He does so in meekness and humility, and because He loves us and wants to spend-time with us. He values us and our friendship, so He has provided a way for us to join with Him in His labors. God does not need us to help Him, but He wants us to help Him and He longs for time with us.

Because God wants us to choose to love Him and choose to be with Him, He doesn't force us to do either. In His astonishing humility, God has bestowed upon sinful, broken men and women the dignity of having roles in shaping history according to the choices they make. God watches patiently as people chart their courses. At crucial times He intervenes with warning or judgment, but always out of love, and gently invites them to turn from the path of destruction and follow His lead. People always are free to accept His invitation or continue on. What we often perceive as harsh or severe actions on God's part, are in reality the actions of a God who perfectly understands the hardness of people's hearts. God acts only to the extent absolutely necessary to get the attention of men and women. If their hearts are very hard, He will increase the severity of the warning or judgment. It is important that we remember, especially when studying the End-Times, that God always warns and brings judgment out of kindness and love, not anger.

God judges to preserve and protect what is good, to remove obstacles to love, and to bring justice by correcting things that are wrong. Again, He never violates our free will. Because people are free to make choices, however, they must live with the consequences of their choices. In the coming day of final judgment, we each will have to answer for every choice we have made, either for or against God.

In Psalm 2 we see a picture of the nations moving and planning together to break away from the rule of God and the One known as "His Anointed," Jesus. The nations in the Psalm are representative of the nations that will exist in the End-Times. The nations in Psalm 2 make a bold declaration, saying, "Let us break Their bonds in pieces and cast away Their cords from us" (Ps. 2:3). The sinful kings and world leaders in the End-Times will make similar declarations that will show their hidden contempt for God and His ways, and will indicate the state of affairs in which the world will be found in the End-Times. The nations of Earth will attempt to separate themselves from biblical morality, and replace it with their own version of morality, which will involve a relativistic celebration of human might and potential. Their vain plots also will involve setting in place their own king to rule the world.

God will see all their plans and the monstrous rage towards Him that lies behind them. He will respond to their schemes in five ways, according to Psalm 2:4-6. First, "He who sits in the heavens shall laugh." Those in power will become intoxicated by their power and importance. Their egos will become inflated because of the immense influence they will have in world affairs. Pride, arrogance and vanity will cause them to make bold declarations of independence and self-determination. God, however, will see the futility of the leaders' efforts, and know they are doomed to fail. He will see it perfectly, even if the saints on Earth do not, and He will not be at all concerned.

Those who don't understand or believe that God's plan will prevail, will see the temporary prosperity of the wicked and manipulative leaders, and will wonder if God doesn't see or care what is happening. Even now, when disaster strikes or trouble comes and we are in despair, our first reaction often is to question whether God sees or cares what is happening. Many give themselves freely to compromise because of their despair, sure that God has abandoned them. The truth is God always sees and always cares about what happens to us. He also knows what evil is being planned against Him and His people, and His first response will be to laugh at their foolish and preposterous plans. Though He will laugh, His laughter will not be out of delight at the choices and plans of the wicked. He will mourn the condition of their hearts and their eventual fates. His laughter will be due to the impossibility that any of those plans could actually work.

The second way God will respond to the schemes of evil men, according to Psalm 2, will be to "hold them in derision." Though the wicked will appear to prosper for a season, God will patiently watch and wait for the right time to unfold His own plan. What may look like inactivity on God's part will not be; nor will His delay be an indication of His approval or emotional distance. God is more emotional than we could ever know or understand. He laughs at the futility of the plans of weak men who are bold in sin, heading for destruction. And He will hold them in derision because of their stubborn, hard-hearted rebellion against His offers of blessing and true life. God's derision speaks of the tone of His laughter. Derision means "contemptuous laughter." The Hebrew word for derision conveys the idea of mocking with babble or unintelligible words, much as someone might contemptuously mock a visitor to their nation who does not speak the language.

It is interesting that God will respond again with babble to the unified efforts of mankind to rebel against Him. The last time people united against God was when they gathered to build a city and a tower "that would reach the top of the heavens" (Gen. 11:4). God's response to their vain and empty plot to exalt and celebrate themselves was to confuse their language. He caused them to babble, and the name of the tower and the evil city that would oppose God came to bear the name "Babble." God accomplished two things by confusing the language of the people. The practical result was that the people's unity was disrupted because they were unable to communicate with one another. Beyond that, God revealed His contemptuous mocking laughter at their foolish pride.

Some interpret God's response as a desperate one due to His fear that their unity would enable them to succeed in their ridiculous scheme. This, however, was not the case. It would have been impossible for anyone to build a tower high enough to reach the top of the heavens. To match the heavenly city described in Revelation 21, these people would have had to build a tower that exceeded 1,500 miles in height. God does not exaggerate, and He has described a city that will come out of Heaven to Earth and will be 1,500 miles high. Human beings begin to feel the limits of the atmosphere at five miles, approximately the height of Mt. Everest. Orbit, or what we call outer space, is reached at 800 miles. The city God will give us in which to live will be beyond anything people could ever attempt to build.

Imagine if every three-year-old in a city gathered together in rage against their parents and defiantly declared a plan to build a skyscraper where they could live apart from their parents. We would consider their plans useless babble. This is what God thought of the plan to build the Tower of Babble. So if this plan was impossible, why did God choose to disrupt the people's unity? He did not use "babble" to frustrate their *task*, but to frustrate their unity in prideful sin and rebellious self-exaltation. Had He not intervened then, sin would have prematurely escalated before the appointed time. The unity of these people would have enabled deep darkness to destroy any hope of redemption.

The Bible speaks of the escalation of sin in the End-Times. Throughout the Bible, there are references to the simultaneous maturation of the Church in righteousness, and the escalation of sin and wickedness in the final generation. God's derision means He will move to frustrate the unity of the sinful nations and their evil agreements. In the right time, He will allow this unity to happen again, allowing sin to return to its former course without it destroying the hope of redemption. While the escalation of sin will come close, Jesus will put an end to it upon His return.

The third way God will respond to the schemes of evil men, according to Psalm 2, will be to "speak to them in His wrath..." When the time is right, God will intervene in world affairs. He will reveal His displeasure with, and His mighty wrath against, wickedness and unrighteousness. He will indeed speak. God has always used prophetic messengers and preachers as a means to speak to His people. Amos 3:7 says, "Surely the Lord God does nothing, unless He reveals His secret to His servants the prophets." God reveals secrets to His messengers, not because He feels He must, but because He wants us to understand that He does nothing in a vacuum. God wants us to understand why our choices and actions matter, and why He responds as He does to them. God gives us divine information so we can consider different options and make better choices. Before any great outbreak of divine judgment, God will always speak to one of His messengers and then send him or her to warn of what is coming.

Right now God is calling and preparing prophetic messengers all over Earth. The End-Times will come soon, and He is preparing people to be messengers, to sound the alarm and warn the Church and the nations. God gives prophetic messengers supernatural insight into His heart and motivations, so they can deliver messages of wrath with tenderness and without accusation. As ambassadors of God, they must precisely and carefully speak as God instructs so they represent Him accurately. In order to fulfill the difficult role of a messenger, their hearts must be closely knit to the heart of God in intimacy and friendship.

In His Word, God spares no details about what will happen in the End-Times for two reasons. First, He wants godly believers to gather and pray for mercy. Second, He wants godly believers to warn the wicked of what will come so they have the opportunity to repent. Joel 2:15 describes prayer meetings, or "sacred assemblies," convened so the godly can contend for mercy and appeal to God to lessen the severity of the coming judgments. Even in His wrath, God speaks clearly and precisely as a good Father, so we have all the information we need to make wise choices about how we spend our time and order our lives.

The fourth way God will respond to the schemes of evil men, according to Psalm 2, will be to "distress them in His deep displeasure." After God speaks warning, He will act. He will not stand by patiently forever. He will act at exactly the right time, and His actions will be perfect. They will produce the most amounts of love and repentance in the hearts of men and women, but will use the least severe means possible to do so. God's judgment is always birthed out of His deep displeasure for wickedness and unrighteousness, but also out of His desire that all people would turn to Him. God's judgment will distress the leaders of the nations and frustrate their plans to replace God's rule with an earthly leader of their choosing. God's judgment on the evil leaders of the world also will play a huge part in accomplishing His plan for the Church. God's shaking of world systems through various natural and supernatural means, also will prepare all the nations to receive God's True King, Jesus.

Jeremiah 25:30-31 communicates the depth and intensity of God's warning and then His actions to distress these nations, kings and leaders: "The Lord will roar from on high, and utter His voice from His holy habitation; He will roar mightily against His fold, He will give a shout, as those who tread the grapes, against all the inhabitants of the earth. A noise will come to the ends of the earth – for the Lord has a controversy with the nations; He will plead his case with all flesh. He will give those who are wicked to the sword..." The imagery speaks of the Lion of the tribe of Judah, Jesus Himself. He will roar as a lion and declare His ultimate victory. His victory is sure. Obtaining it will be as effortless for Him as a person treading grapes. Before His final battle to settle this controversy, Jesus will plead His case to all people, hoping to win their hearts. He will desperately fight to deliver as many as possible from the sword of judgment before He executes final judgment.

God will prepare Earth to be led by Jesus. In some ways, He has been preparing the world to follow His Son for thousands of years. As the Second Coming draws nearer, however, the activities of God's preparation will become more intense. Lines will be drawn more clearly and all will have to choose whether or not they will join the family of God. Many will join, but many will be offended and refuse to join. Natural disasters, wars, famine, widespread death, and supernatural shaking will all grow more intense as time runs out for people to decide their courses. It will be a time of great distress to "all the inhabitants of the earth." Even now, time is of the essence. Psalm 2 is clear about the End-Times. The nations will completely reject God's leadership and sovereignty and fully embrace darkness and wickedness.

As God expresses His displeasure by bringing the greatest shaking in history, most will grow either in their hatred of God or their love for Him. The distress of the shaking will reveal many things. It will become clear who loves God and who hates Him, as well as what God loves and what He hates. God will make very clear what delights Him and what displeases Him in order to clarify the battle lines for the final conflict between Jesus and the nations. As God's plan for the world unfolds, the only people who benefit will be those who have chosen and continue to choose wisely.

God's instruction to everyone has always been to make wise choices. "Now therefore, be wise, O kings; be instructed, you judges of the earth. Serve the Lord with fear, and rejoice with trembling. Kiss the Son, lest He be angry, and you perish in the way, when His wrath is kindled but a little. Blessed are all those who put their trust in Him" (Ps. 2:10-12). We must embrace the wisdom of God and gain the proper perspective of reality. As God prepares the world for the rule of the Great King, it is wisdom for us to serve and embrace that King now in intimacy and rejoicing, rather than to kindle His wrath. It always will be better to trust Him, and not lean on our own understanding, regardless of how bad things get. Jesus is the Anointed One, the blessed Leader. We cannot improve upon His leadership. If we try to do so, we will become like the doomed leaders and kings who will reject Him and attempt to take matters into their own hands. As they wrestle for control and the right to control their own destinies, they will seek to remove every obstacle, the ultimate obstacle being God Himself. They will discover that attempting to remove God as leader will cause them to lose all control and will accelerate their own destruction.

The fifth way God will respond to the schemes of evil men, according to Psalm 2, will be to give the entire Earth to Jesus. "Yet I have set My King on My holy hill of Zion...You are My Son, today

I have begotten You. Ask of Me, and I will give you the nations for Your inheritance, and the ends of the earth for Your possession." Once God's plan for Earth is fully revealed, all Jesus will have to do is ask, and God will give Him the nations to rule. The God of the universe longs to give the nations to His Son. The full destinies of the nations rest in the hands of Jesus, who was begotten, or manifested, in the flesh. Paul said, "Without controversy great is the mystery of godliness: God was manifested in the flesh, justified in the Spirit, seen by angels, preached among the Gentiles, believed on in the world, received up in glory" (1 Tim. 3:16). That God became flesh for the sake of love and to identify with us is an incredible mystery; but this mystery also contains the greatness of the world's destiny in God's glorious plan. The mystery of godliness is wrapped up in what Paul calls "the mystery of His will," or the ultimate purpose of God for all the nations. In light of this mystery, the significance of Jesus ruling Earth after He returns becomes clear. This mystery is the reason the Father and Son labor, and why they are intent on incorporating us into their plan.

The ultimate plan of God is to "gather together in one all things in Christ, both which are in heaven and which are on earth, in Him" (Eph. 1:10). This means the ultimate goal of God's plan is to bring Heaven and Earth together in Jesus. Jesus spoke about this "restoration of all things" in Matthew 17:11, as did Peter in Acts 3:21. The restoration of all things will satisfy God's longing to relate to men and women face to face again, as He did in the Garden of Eden long ago. Joining the realms of Heaven (the supernatural spirit realm of divine power and presence) and Earth (the natural physical realm of human emotions and sensation) will enable God to live together with us again, for all eternity.

God purposefully created the universe with two realms. The material world expresses the glory of the Lord (Rom. 1:20), but is inferior to the spirit world (Heb. 11:3). According to Paul, we will be given resurrected bodies so we can inherit something incorruptible: the Kingdom of God in fullness (1 Cor. 15:50). Our resurrected bodies will facilitate our interaction with the heavenly realm in all of its glory.

Currently, believers are received in Heaven without a material body because they do not need one there. But when Heaven and Earth are joined, we will need resurrected bodies to exist in the Kingdom of God. Jesus will not claim only the physical ground, but will restore Earth, subdue it, and fill it with the glory of His Father. He will bring all people and nations into agreement with God, heal them and prepare them to interact with His Father. And those who have endured will receive their resurrected bodies and will have the privilege of working with Jesus as He restores and subdues Earth and fills it with glory. We will get to help Him make His Father's dream a reality.

The healing, equipping, discipling and preparation of the world will be a progressive work, not an instantaneous one, and will last for one thousand years. After Jesus and the saints have ruled Earth for a millennium, Jesus will give the Kingdom to His Father. The people of Earth will be ready and the last enemy of God, death, will have been conquered (1 Cor. 15:24-28). The people living on Earth will enjoy a thousand years of perfect leadership, as Jesus prepares them for the manifest presence of God's glory to fill the Earth. Only Jesus, who is fully God and fully Man, has the capacity to restore all things, and bring together the fullness of Heaven and of Earth. Jesus can exist and move in both realms and will therefore lead the nations into this fullness with might, glory, power, riches, wisdom and blessing (Rev. 5:12).

END-TIMES
simplified:

CHAPTER SIX:

Satan's Great Plan to Maintain Control

While God's ultimate plan for the world in the age to come is glorious and wonderful, the short-term destiny of the nations is not. Satan, the enemy of God and man, desires a prize, just as God does. The prize he hopes to win is a permanent position of earthly power and control. Satan has had control of the world and its people since Adam and Eve sinned in the Garden of Eden, and he will fight to maintain his control. In choosing the way of sin over obedience to the Lord, mankind gave the world over to Satan's control at the time of the Fall, and continues to give him power and influence to this day. Satan has authority because sinful, carnal people have given it to him and he works furiously to exercise and maintain it.

Jesus called Satan the "ruler of this world" (John 12:31; 14:30; 16:11); and Paul called Satan the "god of this world" (2 Cor 4:4) and the "prince of the power of the air" (Eph. 2:2). The apostle John said the "whole world lies under the sway of the wicked one" (1 John 5:19). Luke 4:5-6 gives an example of Satan's power, power so great he offered it to Jesus: "The devil, taking Him up on a high mountain, showed Him all the kingdoms of the world...The devil said to Him, 'All this authority I will give You...for this has been delivered to me, and I give it to whomever I wish.'" Jesus didn't contend with Satan then, but both understood that Satan's position was the present reality and that all would be changed at the Second Coming of Jesus. Thus Jesus was not threatened by Satan's control or bothered by the offer. He and His Father have always had a plan to take back what is His, but Jesus has always been committed to doing it His Father's way, through meekness, pain and enduring hardship. Satan's temptation was to offer Jesus an easy path to rule the world, without the pain of the cross. This temptation was not easy for Jesus to refuse, as the Bible relates in describing Jesus later in the Garden of Gethsemane.

Though Satan's power is great, it is not greater than God's. God is always aware of Satan's plans and actions, and is not threatened by them. God has always been, is now, and will always be in control of the universe. But as the sovereign leader of history, He has given us the dignity of choosing our path and our king, and deciding whom we will allow to rule our lives. If we choose to continue walking "according to the course of this world" (Eph. 2:2), we will remain in the kingdom of darkness, under Satan's rule.

If we choose God's rule, however, He will pick us up out of the dirty, dark "river" of this world and set us into a different one, which the Bible calls "the river of life" (Ezek. 47:1-12; Rev. 22:2). Once we are set into this river, our lives will be on radically different courses than before. We will grow in the light and the life of Jesus.

Most people are not aware they are swimming in the river that will lead to destruction. They have never considered Satan to be their king. Satan, however, has given much thought to the issue of kingship. He knows the Bible predicts his eventual doom and torment. He is fully aware of the prophetic promises in the Bible, but he is somehow blind to or unwilling to accept the reality of his certain downfall, and refuses to give up. There is no contest between Satan and the all-encompassing power of our God; but in his outrageous arrogance and pride, Satan will nonetheless attempt to outmaneuver God and maintain his power base. Satan's plan involves two main strategies. The first is to wipe out the objects of God's prophetic promises, the Christians and the Jews (Rev. 12:17). The second is to set his own man in place as king of the world. The Bible calls Satan's would-be king the Antichrist.

To many, Antichrist is at best a fable, a creation of biblical conspiracy theorists and novelists. Tales of a crazed king, filled with lust for world domination, make easy targets for those who don't subscribe to a "doom and gloom" mentality. The prophetic writers of the Bible, however, did not view the traumatic events of the End-Times or the horrific nature of the Antichrist as part of a "doom and gloom" mentality. They simply accepted them as being part of the reality that would come to the sinful, rebellious world, which had rejected the leadership of God.

As we prepare for the End-Times, it is important to study the Antichrist and his role. The Bible discusses the Antichrist and his activities frequently and in detail. The Holy Spirit gives much attention and prominence to the subject. The Antichrist's title, the "man of sin" (2 Thess. 2:3), speaks of a two-fold reality. He will be the personification of evil and the personification of that which appeals to the carnal nature of man. Evil and wickedness by nature are self-exalting. The result of people's self exaltation is a self-promoting, self-seeking society in which people seek to receive glory from other people. We tend to think of evil in the overt expressions of darkness we find repulsive. We don't realize that much of what God despises is what mankind values most. Jesus said in Luke 16:15, "You are those who justify yourselves before men, but God knows your hearts. For what is highly esteemed among men is an abomination in the sight of God."

Studying the Antichrist will prepare us to face his rise to power. His domination of the world scene will be part of the End-Times suffering. As we learn what the Bible says about him, the Holy Spirit will impart the wisdom and revelation necessary for us to oppose him.

To study the Antichrist is to study evil incarnate. It is also to explore the depths of sin in the heart of every person, including our own. Antichrist will personify all of the sinful lusts and ambitions of the nations and will embody all that carnally-minded men and women esteem, in that he will be appealing to many because of his gifts, skills, charisma and power. There are many outward things we admire in those men and women we perceive as being great; but those attributes only seem great because our unrenewed minds love earthly things, not godly things. We don't realize the magnitude of our depravity, but through the Antichrist, God will make clear that the things mankind exalts, God despises. As we become aware of and accept our inherent depravity, we will recognize our need for God. As we cry out to Him and submit to Him, we will begin, by His grace, to live holy and righteous lives. Our lives will serve as examples to others and we will be able to speak the truth of Jesus into their lives and help them to make right choices now and in the End-Times.

So we know both God and Satan are working to draw people to them. As clear battle lines are drawn in the End-Times, both will look for loyal followers. Both will determine who stands with them, and attempt to recruit those who don't. The difference is that God loves everyone and wants everyone to choose to run with and to Him in love. Satan, on the other hand, hates everyone. He has no use for people beyond his wicked and brutal self-serving plans. People quickly outlive their usefulness to him and he quickly discards them. While his initial plan will be to kill all Christians and Jews, the people of promise, his ultimate desire is to eliminate the entire human race, every member of which was made in God's image. Those who join with Satan will not find in him a friend, but their worst enemy, an enemy fully committed to destroying them.

Satan's hatred of men and women and his scheme to destroy them began long ago. In the Garden of Eden, he took the form of a serpent and shrewdly deceived Adam and Eve by convincing them that God, with whom they enjoyed face-to-face fellowship, wasn't all He appeared to be. He persuaded them that God had withheld true blessing from them, so they began to question God's goodness. Satan told Adam and Eve they could attain wisdom and find satisfaction apart from God, and has told the same lie to men and women ever since. He has propagated the idea that there exists wisdom superior to God's Word and has tempted mankind to seek it. People have continued to believe the lie that there exists wisdom superior to God's and the lie that God doesn't have their best interests in mind. The result is that we attempt to take care of ourselves, rather than placing ourselves in God's care and doing things His way. In our pride, we think we know better than God what is best for us. Once we reject the truth that we need God and His help, we give ourselves over to our own ways, and thus remove ourselves from God's protection. When we step out from under God's protection and care, Satan can easily manipulate us for his own benefit. He sends his demonic minions to control all the areas of our hearts and minds that have become open doors to darkness and sin.

Through this deception, Satan has ensnared the hearts of men and women, and established an evil world system that kills, steals and destroys countless people's lives. Evil is steadily increasing as Earth moves towards the "fullness of transgressions" (Dan. 8:23). The nations are falling into line with Satan's plan and the conditions are ripe for his next move, which will be attempting to establish his kingship. By "fullness of transgressions" the Bible doesn't mean sin itself will get worse. Sin has existed since the Fall and has always destroyed lives. Sin cannot "grow worse." Transgression reaching its fullness means people will unify in their sin as never before. When people gather and agree in and with sin, a social context will be created that gives license to all the evil imaginings and desires in people's hearts and minds.

When sin remains hidden, there is an illusion of mankind's goodness and decency. For example, right now it is socially unacceptable in our society to discuss many of the dark things lurking in people's hearts. But things are changing. Right before our eyes, barriers are crumbling under the weight of "freedom of expression." Darker and darker expressions of sin are becoming socially acceptable. The sin that has resided in the hearts of men and women since the Fall is now being expressed in the light of day. The unity in sin that will prepare the way for the Antichrist is even now fast solidifying and will become completely so in the End-Times. Because Satan's plan depends entirely on mankind's cooperation with his agenda, it is people who will empower the Antichrist to rule, not Satan.

Antichrist will be the chief player in Satan's plan to maintain his rule of Earth. The Bible describes the Antichrist as the one who will be free to murder the saints of God, to blaspheme, to "corrupt with flattery" those who do wickedly (Dan. 11:32), and to brutally enforce loyalty with minimal reward (Rev. 13:15). It says he will put into action this plan with bitterness, anger, deceit, betrayal, trouble and ruthless ambition (Ps. 10:7-11). The Antichrist will have freedom to act this way because the standards and conditions of the times will have made it socially acceptable for him to do so. People will continue to empower and give permission to greater and greater expressions of sin and darkness, and thus will establish Satan's power base for him. From that power base, Satan will gain the platform he needs to enact a systematic eradication of all Christians and Jews.

The Rise of the Antichrist Empire

The Bible is not clear about the origin of Antichrist, who will carry out the final, desperate phases of Satan's plan. We don't know definitely where he will come from. Many murderous dictators of the past seemed to arise from nowhere and lay hold of power and influence overnight. So it may be with Antichrist. There is much mystery surrounding this future world leader, who John described as the "beast that was, and is not, and yet is" (Rev. 17:8). Antichrist's identity has been the subject of numerous discussions and debates and many don't know what to make of him. We know he will "ascend out of the bottomless pit and go to perdition" and will cause many who dwell on Earth to marvel when they see him (Rev. 17:8). Regardless of where he will come from, when Antichrist arrives on the scene, he will make a huge, international impact. Daniel 9:27 says of Antichrist that "he shall confirm a covenant with many" for seven years. Isaiah calls this a "covenant with death" and an "agreement with Sheol" (Is. 28:18). Israel will be one of the "many" nations who participate in this covenant, which will be portrayed as a peace treaty. Israel will be fooled into making a deal with Antichrist, who will appear to exude wisdom and goodness (Ps. 36:3), though wickedness and deceit will be in his heart. As a result, Israel will lower her defenses and rest in what will appear to be peace and safety from the continual waves of attack that have wearied her people (Ezek. 38:11; 1 Thess. 5:3). Because Antichrist's agreement will be with "many," it will appear that peace and safety have become a global reality for the first time. Though the peace will be false, it will satisfy the many people living in constant fear of terror attack, war and rumors of war.

The world at that time already will have begun the transition from what Jesus called "birth pangs" to the next prophetic stage. The process will not have entered the "heavy labor" phase of the Great Tribulation, when the "water will break" and a flood of trouble will come to Earth. It will be a far more subtle and dangerous phase of history. Antichrist will be only a regional leader with a growing international prominence. His rise, according to the angelic messenger of Daniel 11:21, will not be immediate. He will come "peaceably" and "seize the kingdom with intrigue." He will initially be part of the coalition of nations propagating the newfound false peace and safety, but will eventually be given power and honor.

As a result of the newfound world-wide peace and safety, a world religion will emerge in the End-Times. Antichrist will begin his rise to power as a key proponent of this religion. According to Revelation 17:3, his early prominence will be tied to this religion in a mysterious way, but he will surely benefit from the network of relational connections and economic prosperity. This same verse says he will allow himself to be the lesser of the two in the relationship for a little while. He will enjoy the way this religion prepares the way for his rise to power by shifting the culture of the world to accommodate his plans. Once this religion has served his purpose, he will turn the tables and destroy it, as we will see in the next chapter.

How will the new religion prepare the way for Antichrist's rise to power and the emergence of his true nature? This world religion, the "Mystery Babylon" woman described in Chapter Two, will embrace and promote "toleration" and world unity. The unity will come at the expense of all whole-hearted and uncompromising expressions of faith, which will be viewed as dangerous and threatening to the peace. This time will be a terrifying and hostile time for passionate believers committed to the truth of God at any cost. The newfound peace will be so tenuous that people will deal brutally with anyone who threatens to disturb it. And though there will be vocal preachers of the truth who disturb it, it will be dangerous and difficult for believers to remain radical, passionate followers of Jesus. It will be seem safer, wiser and even more loving to embrace the culture of "tolerance."

Even now, we see hints of this. "Open-mindedness," which can be defined as accepting everything and anything as true, is tolerated and even encouraged. Yet, there is little tolerance for those who consider the Word of God to be absolutely true. Speaking about God or a god or discussing "spirituality" is acceptable to almost everyone. But these "safe" topics have much more to do with a humanistic god defined by the people, rather than the true God of Scripture. Religion has become about pleasing and gratifying self. Attaining inner peace, prosperity, contentment, comfort and happiness, as defined by each individual, is considered the highest goal.

This idea of deciding for oneself what will "work" as far as religion goes, is paving the way for the religion of tolerance that will emerge. At its core, this new religion will hold the real promise of wealth and financial blessing. The luxury that enthrones the "harlot" of religion in Revelation 17:4 is a picture of the promise of prosperity the new religion will make. The message of prosperity will please carnal men and women, the "lovers of pleasure" and self Paul describes in 2 Timothy 3:1-5. Our generation is already "heaping up for itself" (2 Tim. 4:3) teachers who will tell us what we want to hear. Anything relating to Christianity that is controversial or uncomfortable is already being set aside and replaced by the "whatever makes you happy is okay" kind of preaching that fills the pews. It seems wiser and kinder to many to embrace any doctrine or faith and encourage everyone to "find their own way to God." The acceptance and propagation of this mindset will worsen and the flow of finances will be intoxicating. The words will sound so wise. When the new religion dominates the scene, anyone preaching an alternative message will be met with hostility and persecuted. Due to the pressure to conform, many in the Church will fall away from the faith during this season, the season just before Antichrist reveals his true nature and intentions (2 Thess. 2:3). Meanwhile, behind the scenes, Antichrist will have been slowly ascending to power, building his resources and amassing his forces. He will have been making the necessary alliances and back door agreements that will propel him into power. Much of the world will have compromised to join this world religion. It will be an easy thing for him to exploit their compromise and entice them to go one step further and worship him as God.

Ezekiel made a frightening statement about Antichrist. He said Antichrist would be "wiser than Daniel" and no secret would be hidden from him (Ezek. 28:3). What makes this so frightening is that Daniel was said to have been "ten times wiser" than the most brilliant, learned men on Earth in his day (Dan. 1:20). That means Antichrist will be unbelievably wise. His unmatchable intellect and mental capacity will propel him to an unprecedented height of power and honor. With his fierce countenance, his grasp of sinister schemes (Dan. 8:23), and his strategic mind, he will outmaneuver anyone who gets in his way, including the kings within his own alliance who might vie for power (Dan. 7:20). He will be the most gifted speaker of his time (Dan. 7:20; Rev.13:2), and will appear to embody the best humanity has to offer.

When we study Antichrist, we must not exalt him or build him up with hype or exaggeration. Though he is Satan's chosen tool, God will be the One allowing him to be raised up so He can bring about His plan. God will allow Antichrist to obtain authority, influence and power. While Satan will give him authority (Rev. 13:2) and men will give him authority (Rev. 13:4), he ultimately wouldn't have any authority if God did not grant it to him (Rev. 13:7). The rise of Antichrist will be part of Satan's plan, but God knows even now exactly what will happen and is already way ahead of Satan. While there are two opposing plans unfolding, there is really but one true plan: God's plan to bring the Church to maturity and at the same time give the nations a clear view of wickedness and righteousness so they might choose now and forever to love Him. Satan's plan will result only in his own destruction.

ENDTIMES
simplified:

CHAPTER SEVEN

The Two Plans Unfold

The Book of Revelation provides much insight into Satan's actions in the End-Times, and makes clear that he is incapable of creating something from nothing. His schemes are wickedly brilliant, but he is no artist. With his limited ability and creativity, Satan is forced to take that which God has created or initiated and counterfeit it. He twists the works of God into enticing imitations to deceive people.

God has created everything to appeal to our spirit, and as our spirits become more alive in God, His ways become more desirable. We become more tender-hearted and grow in love as we submit to the glorious process God has set into place for our lives. At last we become possessed by the very Spirit of God, and our hearts are fully knit with His. For we have been bought with His blood, and we are the inheritance the Father gives the Son (Eph. 1:17-19), and the desire of God is to make this a living reality.

Satan, on the other hand, shapes his counterfeit expressions to appeal to our sinful, carnal nature. What Satan presents to us is designed to ensnare and deceive us and guide us down the path that leads to hardness, bitterness and destruction. His goal is for us to become fully given over to darkness and thus open the door to possession of another kind: demonic bondage, which will render us helpless against the "flaming arrows" of the enemy (Eph. 6:16). Over time, if we remain open to evil, we will become fully knit to darkness.

The reason Satan wants to eliminate the human race is because He wants to eliminate the Kingdom of God. God wants to cleanse the world of wickedness and darkness. Satan wants to cleanse the world of all who are part or will be part of God's Kingdom. He will work furiously to eliminate all those who oppose him and draw everyone else to him. Satan's desire is to reign on Earth forever, so he will work to create the optimal conditions for his own kingdom on Earth, which involves destroying mankind and the Kingdom of God.

Once Antichrist has set in place the new religion and begun the mass murder of Jews and Christians, he will entice the nations with prosperity and "false" signs and wonders (Rev. 13:13) tied to the new religion. The signs and wonders will be real, but not true. They will be demonically empowered, not Holy Spirit empowered. They will seem so true, however, that Jesus said they could "deceive, if possible, even the elect" (Matt. 24:24). Antichrist will create a false worship and prayer movement and attempt to force all men and women to join. He will present himself as a "more appealing" god offering more promise to humanity than God. The preaching ministry of Antichrist will invite everyone to embark on a journey of making themselves gods. To make his invitation credible, Antichrist will offer it only after he has become a global dictator with more power than any leader before him. Over a three-and-a-half-year period, Antichrist will consolidate his power base and set the stage for the next phase of Satan's plan.

The Dramatic Event

At precisely the right moment, Antichrist will capitalize on the optimal global conditions and act on the true ambitions of his wicked heart. Having worked behind the scenes for years to build his political and military power base, the time will come when he will have no more need for the false religious system. Revelation 17:13 describes this time as being when ten kings in alliance with Antichrist and one another and having "one mind...will give their power and authority to the beast." The leaders will hand over all governmental authority to the one man among them, Antichrist, who can take over the city of Babylon and its religious and economic resources, and establish the ten-nation empire as the one global power.

When Babylon is taken over, the stage will be almost set for Antichrist's dramatic event: the "abomination of desolation" (Dan. 9:27; Matt. 24:15). But there will be one more event yet to take place before the abomination of desolation. Satan will be cast down from the heavenly realm and war will break out in Heaven (Rev. 12:7). The angel who spoke to Daniel described this event saying, "At that time Michael shall stand up, the great prince who watches over your people; and there shall be a time of trouble, such as never was since there was a nation..." (Dan. 12:1). Revelation 12:7-17 says when Michael, the great archangel who protects Israel, stands up with his angels to fight the "dragon," who is Satan, and his angels, Satan's forces will not prevail. Not only will the forces of Satan lose the fight, but there will be no "place found for them in heaven any *only after the battle?* longer."

One of the Bible's titles for Satan is "accuser of our brethren" (Rev. 12:10). He has constantly accused believers before God day and night, throughout all of history. The story of Job is an example of Satan accusing the brethren before God. Satan accused Job before the Father, and continually reminded God of Job's unworthiness to inherit the promised kingdom. In Satan's mind, the "brethren," the saints of God, are unworthy to hold such a privileged position, so he will continue to accuse us night and day until he is cast down, and then his accusations will cease. He will no longer have access to God before the throne, for the testimony of the Lord will be the final word about the Church. "Now salvation, and strength, and the kingdom of our God, and the power of His Christ have come, for the accuser of our brethren, who accused them before our God day and night, has been cast down. And they [the saints] overcame him by the blood of the Lamb and by the word of their testimony, and they did not love their lives to the death. Therefore rejoice, O heavens, and you who dwell in them!" (Rev. 12:10-12). Heaven will rejoice at the Church's victory over her great enemy, and the silencing of his accusations against her. It will be a glorious moment. There will also be, however, a terrifying dimension to this moment.

While the heavens rejoice, Earth and all its inhabitants will experience a time of terrible woe when Satan is cast down to Earth. Scripture says of that time, "for the devil has come down to you, having great wrath, because he knows he has a short time" (Rev. 12:12). When Michael stands up (Dan. 12:1), it will signal the beginning of the most troublesome time in history for Israel and for all the nations: the Great Tribulation. Satan will come to Earth with a new and heightened expression of rage. His rage will be born of desperation, the kind of rage a cornered animal feels when it knows its end is near. It will be the most terrible kind of rage, a fearsome and brutal one. All of Satan's plans to maintain control will be accelerated. He will know his heavenly campaign against the saints has failed, and his last chance to wage war against God will be through the nations. He will attempt to eradicate every Christian and Jew who could potentially receive the Kingdom of God (Rev. 12:17).

When Satan comes to Earth to wage war, the stage will be set for the final battle. Antichrist will have stealthily secured his military and political might. He and his allies, the ten kings, will destroy the city of Babylon, seize her economic resources and move to crush her religious sphere of influence. He will move to crush the global religious system to establish himself as the true God. To legitimize his apparent and deceptive divine nature before the people, Satan will make a chilling decision: he will give the Antichrist his "power, his throne, and great authority" (Rev. 13:2). Antichrist will then have governmental authority over the entire demonic realm, all spiritual power in the kingdom of darkness. It will be then that he reveals his true nature and his unbelievably wicked and deranged beliefs. He will present himself to the world as being God Himself.

In his second letter to the Thessalonians, Paul called Antichrist the son of perdition "who opposes and exalts himself above all that is called God or that is worshipped, so that he sits as God in the temple of God, showing himself that he is God" (verse 2:4). Antichrist will have partnered with Babylon for years as he rose to power, using her as she used him, but all the while hating her and despising the watered-down phoniness she represented. Antichrist will have always believed that he was the true God, the only one worth worshipping. Though deceived, he will see through the false piety of the self-serving religious system and its innate emptiness. After all, he will reason, if they (Mystery Babylon) aren't worshipping him, who are they worshipping? This question will cause his contempt for her to grow over the years of their pretended partnership. In the same way, Hitler professed a love for the Church in Germany as he attempted to use her influence and wealth to accomplish his goals. Over time, however, his true contempt for the Church became evident.

Having always believed he was God, Antichrist will next set out to prove his deity to the world. After he destroys Babylon, he will bring an end to the Hebrew sacrifices, which will have been restarted in the rebuilt temple in Jerusalem (Dan. 9:27). Antichrist will have other plans for the temple, plans involving an unthinkable act of arrogance. He will set up an image of himself in the Holy of Holies and demand that the nations worship it. This event is what Jesus called the abomination of desolation.

This image of Antichrist will appear to be living (Rev. 13:15). The deceived people on Earth will make duplicate images of the Antichrist and place them throughout the nations. Each duplicate image will also appear to be alive. The images will speak and somehow cause the deaths of many who refuse to worship the Antichrist. Revelation 13 explains how Antichrist will gain the authority to make such demands and carry out his evil plan. The apostle John, author of Revelation, saw in a vision what will take place. First, John saw that Antichrist will be mortally wounded with a traumatic head wound (Rev. 13:3). He will be "wounded by the sword and live" (Rev. 13:14). Though deadly, his wound will be dramatically healed. All will witness this miraculous display of supernatural power, and the event will shock the world. John said the entire world will marvel, and Antichrist will develop a worldwide following. His fame will be great and his legitimacy as God will be established in the minds of many people. When he goes out to make war among the nations, he will be thought of as an unbeatable enemy (Rev. 13:4), and many will choose to worship him, rather than fight against him.

The False Worship and Prayer Movement

Satan's next desperate and twisted move will be to deceive and force millions of people into joining a false worship movement. The movement will be orchestrated by a second "beast," the "False Prophet" (Rev. 13:11-18). The False Prophet will speak gentle words that mask demonic hatred and possess "all the authority of the first beast in his presence" (Rev. 13:12). The False Prophet will cause "all the earth and those who dwell in it to worship the first beast," Antichrist (Rev. 13:12). The False Prophet also will function like a "false Holy Spirit" in a counterfeit trinity. Satan will play the part of the Father, Antichrist will appear to be the Son, and the False Prophet will function as the Holy Spirit. Millions will be enticed and deceived into joining the false worship movement. Those who aren't lured into joining, will be pressured to join, with the penalty for refusing to join being death.

Those who willingly join in worshipping Antichrist will be given a mark (Rev. 13:16-17), which will enable them to participate in the global economic system. This mark will be a counterfeit of the mark of God described in Revelation 7:3-4, given to those who are loyal to Him, according to 2 Chronicles 16:9: "For the eyes of the LORD run to and fro throughout the whole earth, to show Himself strong on behalf of those whose heart is loyal to Him." Another example of the mark of God is described in Ezekiel. "...And He called to the man clothed with linen, who had the writer's inkhorn at his side; and the LORD said to him, 'Go through the midst of the city, through the midst of Jerusalem, and put a mark on the foreheads of the men who sigh and cry over all the abominations that are done within it'" (Ezek. 9:3-4).

Believers will be protected by God's seal of divine protection when His wrath breaks out on Earth. Paul said in his first letter to the Thessalonians that "God did not appoint us to wrath" (1 Thess. 5:9). When the wrath of God is poured out on Earth in judgment, it will not be directed at believers. It will be directed at the wicked who despise God and His ways. He will place a seal of protection on His own and keep us safe from His wrath. Psalm 91 lays out the principle that we will find safety and refuge in our God during times of trouble. "He will give His angels charge over you," is the promise of that passage. Those who "set their love upon" Him will be delivered, and "set on high."

There is a difference, however, between the wrath of God, which is directed only at the wicked, and the wrath of Satan, which is directed at everyone. Having God's seal of protection from His wrath doesn't mean we will experience no hardship, trials, or martyrdom in the end-time tribulation. Finding refuge in the Lord does not mean our lives will be trouble-free or care-free. What it does mean is that during the storms that will come, we can find refuge and safety in Him, and know that while we may experience trouble for a moment, our eternal and glorious destiny with Him is certain (2 Cor. 4:17). In fact, the coming trouble will work eternal glory in us for the age to come. The Great Tribulation will come and will be experienced by believers because believers will be Satan's prime targets. So, while we are immune to the wrath of God, God will allow and empower Satan to bring his wrath upon us. God will allow this, not because He is angry with us, but because He loves us. He will use the fire of Satan's wrath to produce "genuine faith" (1 Peter 1:7), which is more precious than gold.

Satan's mark will be given to those who willingly and wholeheartedly worship Antichrist. It will be a seal of approval not easily obtained. Nobody will "accidentally" acquire this mark. It will only be given to those who choose to bow down in worship and pledge allegiance and complete loyalty to Antichrist. This mark will be a type of "passport" for its recipients, giving them access to all kinds of privileges in the Antichrist kingdom and other territories under his influence. Buying and selling without this mark will be difficult. The marks of both God and Satan will be "loyalty marks," to clearly delineate what side people are on, and remove ambiguity and grey areas of lukewarm, non-committal lifestyles. Both sides want radical commitment and to eliminate the middle-of-the-road people.

The faith of the saints will be tested, as we wonder where our provision will come from, and we will have to trust God for the impossible more than ever. Much will be at stake in that time, and anyone who buckles under the pressure and worships the "beast" to receive the short-term benefits, will "drink of the wine of the wrath of God" in the fullness of its strength (Rev. 14:10).

The wrath of God will be great against those who compromise, take the mark, and worship the beast, because the choice to do so will be a purposeful and deliberate one. Proving loyalty to Antichrist by taking the mark will not be a minor decision. People will have to fully convert and commit to follow Antichrist before they will be given the mark. The pressure to make this decision will be intense, but not impossible to resist.

Resistance to Antichrist will be punishable by death; so many believers will be martyred as the result of their resistance. The conditions for this wave of martyrdom will have been established during the first phase of Satan's plan, the new and false world religion. Through its deceptive and sinister ministry, the world religion will have established a global culture of martyrdom, and thus paved the way for increased levels of martyrdom to be socially and culturally acceptable. After Antichrist reveals his true nature and proclaims that he is God, the groundwork laid over the previous three and a half years will facilitate this wide-spread martyrdom during the next few years. The persecution and martyrdom of believers will be more extreme and pervasive than ever before. Everything Antichrist accomplishes will be allowed by God. God will always be in control. Chapter Four of Revelation is meant to establish and reiterate that it is God who is in command of the past, the present and the future. The throne and might of Satan are nothing compared to the matchless splendor of the mighty King. The next move will be God's. He will have been watching and waiting as Satan's plan seemed to prevail. But the trap will be already set, and the conditions for God's ultimate victory will be in place. Revelation Five describes what will happen next. God will be ready to hand over the rule and leadership of the world to His worthy Son, the only human King worthy to receive it. The catalyst for this moment will be the readiness of the Church to stand with Jesus as He receives the world from His Father. As Satan conceived and carried out his plan, God will have secretly unfolded His. Having known a time of martyrdom on an unimaginable scale would come, God will have set out beforehand to ready His Church for that hour. What many would call the darkest hour in the Church's history has been ordained by God to be her finest.

END-TIMES
simplified:

CHAPTER EIGHT:

The Emergence of the Victorious Church

While the crowning of Antichrist as king and God will be dramatic and significant, an even more dramatic event will take place in the throne room of Heaven. God will give His Son a scroll. This event will be so momentous the angels around the throne of God will break into a new song. The angels have sung a song of praise to the King for an untold amount of time, night and day; but a new song will break out, a powerful, glorious song that marks a turning point in the course of history. This new song will mark the beginning of the sequence of events that will culminate in the return of Jesus to Earth and the full establishment of His Kingdom.

This celebration of the angels is one in which we will eventually participate and enjoy forever. Imagine ten thousand times ten thousand angels, with "thousands of thousands" more, singing and thundering with voices more beautiful than those in the best choirs on Earth. The angels will rejoice and revel in that moment, for they will know what glory is in store for the saints. God gives us this chapter of the Bible to calm our fearful hearts and remind us that His plan is perfect. He knows the whole story, including Antichrist's claim to be God, and He is untroubled by Satan's doomed plan.

The scroll God will present to Jesus represents God's leadership over history and is the "title deed" to Earth. It will contain God's plan to bring to a close mankind's current earthly existence and usher in the age to come (Rev. 5:1-14). We know this because of the events that are described in the following chapters of Revelation. The scroll will have remained in God's hands until someone is found worthy to take it. As the only One found worthy, Jesus will take the scroll, break its seals and unveil its contents.

As Jesus comes forward to take the scroll, there will be a dramatic shift and much movement in the heavenly court. As He takes hold of the scroll, the final moments of history will begin. God's preparation of His people will be coming to completion. Behind the scenes, as Satan has gone about his own business, God will have been preparing His people to take over the government of the world, and function in meekness and humility as kings and priests. God's "secret weapon," an authentic worship and prayer movement, will be unleashed on the kingdom of darkness. In one accord, the Church will praise His ways and release His judgment through intercession. The unveiling of Jesus' singing, praying Bride will surprise the nations and dismay Satan.

So the shift will begin with the release of the new song of the Lord in Heaven and Earth mentioned earlier. There are many verses in the Bible describing this new song. The new song will not be a new "sound," but rather worship that reflects God's new activity on Earth. As this new expression of God's heart is released from Heaven to Earth, the Church will sing in agreement. Isaiah 42:10-13 gives a preview: "Sing to the Lord a new song, and His praise to the ends of the earth…let them give glory to the Lord, and declare His praise to the coastlands. The Lord shall go forth like a mighty man of war. He shall cry out, yes, shout aloud; He shall prevail against His enemies."

Prophetic singing has always been one of God's most powerful weapons. He uses it to release His power on Earth, and will use it as such in the End-Times. The power of prophetic singing is not found in the songs themselves, but in the way they knit our hearts with the heart of God and facilitate unity among believers. As the new song at the end of the age breaks forth, believers will share God's heart and be unified with one another. We will sing in agreement and praise of Jesus' role as the Judge preparing to loose judgments on Earth. The end-time Church will be led by prophetic singers, singing in concert with the Holy Spirit about the coming judgments of the Lord. The Church will be in full agreement with His methodology and leadership, and will in essence sing passionately together this theme: "We agree with who you are, O Judge of the earth!"

Even now, God is orchestrating a new level of worship and prayer to unite His people with His heart and with our fellow believers. This unity will be directly related to the new level of power He will release to usher in a Great Harvest of souls and the Second Coming of His Son. Having anointed prophetic singers, who are sensitive to the Holy Spirit and skilled in engaging and emboldening a body of believers, will be critical to the fulfillment of God's plan.

Just as the victorious Church at the end of the age will be a singing Church, it will be a praying Church. It is just as important for the end-time Church to be fully committed to a lifestyle of prayer and fasting as it is for it to be engaged in prophetic worship. Right now, God is initiating such a prayer and fasting movement in the world-wide Body of Christ. Prayer and song are the two main vehicles by which God molds and shapes our hearts into agreement with Him. The full bowls of Revelation 5:8 speak of the prayers of the saints. As we pray, those bowls are capturing each and every prayer. When they are full, the Church will have matured as a praying Bride.

The Church's maturing process will have been birthed in the early stages of God's final plan, during His purifying shaking before the Great Tribulation. The Church will be mature and prepared before Antichrist becomes a powerful global dictator. Before Antichrist puts himself in place, the Church will emerge as a unified, fiery and mature body of believers. The world will witness an expression of Christianity from this body radically different than what we know today. It is part of Jesus' strategy to lead His Bride through testing at the hands of those who seek to destroy her, the false trinity of Satan, Antichrist, and the False Prophet. This radically different expression of Christianity will only come about as a result of the Bride's testing and victory during this time. It will be God orchestrating the cosmic drama, and He will know there are real lives in the balance. But as a jealous, fiery God, He will do whatever He must do to present His Son with a worthy, equally-yoked Bride to enjoy forever. Many will fall away and fail the test. Many will not like His leadership and will reject Him. Those who don't, however, will receive great reward at the Second Coming of Jesus.

Judgment Begins in God's House

Before judgment comes to the nations of the Earth, it will come to the house of the Lord, the Church. Referring to the Church, Peter warned, "it begins with us first" (1 Pet. 4:17). The Lamb of God, Jesus, will be in full agreement and partnership with His Father as He initiates final judgment. Before He shakes Earth, he will shake the Church, shaking all that can be shaken (Heb. 12:25-29; Hag. 2:6-7). The Church will be tried and tested at the hands of the "counterfeit bride," the new mystery religion of false peace and prosperity described in Revelation 17. Everyone in the Church will be forced to choose to which "bride" they will give themselves. They will have two choices: the Bride of Christ, the body of believers aligned with God; or the counterfeit bride, the body of people given to the global, compromised religion based on false promises of peace, safety and personal happiness.

God will shake every dimension of our earthly existence with His judgments. His hope and desire is for all people to turn to the "Desire of the Nations" (Hag. 2:7). In that hour He will "speak from heaven" (Heb. 12:25) and we must not refuse Him. He wants to shake all that can be shaken in order to remove from us anything that might hinder our love for Him. He wants to purify us. We must be unshakable in order to receive His Kingdom, a "kingdom that cannot be shaken" (verse 27). God is a "consuming fire" (verse 29), who will move jealously to purify believers in that hour (Dan. 11:35; 12:10). The saints will be refined and made white, spotless in His sight and fit to rule with Him (Eph. 5:26-27). God will sanctify and cleanse His bride with the water of the Word, "that He might present her to Himself a glorious church" (Eph. 5:27).

Believers who take offence at God and His plan, those who have "shakable" lives, will fall away (Matt. 24:10-12; 2 Thess. 2:3). False prophets will deceive many and God Himself will release a strong delusion as many unrepentantly buy into Satan's deception (2 Thess. 2:11). Believers who stand fast will be viewed as disruptive influences, targeted for elimination, and martyred by political regimes eager to maintain the tenuous peace of the day (Rev. 17:6). Rather than hindering the quickly-maturing global prayer movement, however, the increase in martyrdom will add fuel to its fire and stir the saints to cry for justice (Rev. 6:9-11). When the trials of global disapproval and martyrdom hit the Church, there will be but two choices for and two reactions among believers. Some will leave and some will pray. The great "falling away" from the faith Paul described in 2 Thessalonians 2:3 will be the result of God's shaking the Church. Anyone who is shaken into offence and bitterness towards God will leave. Those who trust His goodness will pray. When those who are offended refuse to pray and turn from the Lord, the prayer movement will come into full maturity, power and authority.

God's prayer movement will be the secret to the Church's strength in the final hours of history. The Lord is inviting this generation, our generation, to enter into a lifestyle of prayer and intercession now. In His wisdom God has ordained prayer and intimacy with Him to be among the best ways to prepare us to endure the storms of life. Those who are diligent in prayer and intercession today, and who become intimate with God as a result, will be among those best equipped to handle the pressures of the coming shaking. God never intended prayer to be merely a value, but a lifestyle. Engaging in continual prayer and fasting means embracing a way of life before the Lord that challenges everything in us. Such a lifestyle presses our sensibilities to their limits. But when we fully embrace this lifestyle, God brings about a significant and glorious transformation in our hearts. When the Church corporately embraces and approaches prayer as a lifestyle and not a meeting, she will begin to take significant steps towards her ultimate destiny, which involves partnering with God to shape history, affect the spiritual atmosphere, and influence nations.

The judgment coming to the Church will ready her to face the End-Times. Through it, God will use the Body of Christ as a fiery, powerful, clear voice in the hour of greatest darkness. When the events of the End-Times are shaking the Earth, God will use the Church to present a chaotic world with an alternative to wickedness and darkness. Through the Church, He will make a way for others to join His stable, steady, unshakable Church, which will be filled with thriving believers in love with Him. Though many in the Church will be slain, they will die with lovesick and fiery hearts. Their witness will astonish the nations.

In its current state of powerlessness and compromise, the Church offers a weak witness to the nations on behalf of God. It is virtually indistinguishable from the many godless organizations in the world. As the Church's leader, Jesus is fully committed to changing this. He will ensure that the Church emerges from her great testing by the world's false religion as a true representation of Him and His heart. The Church will come forth as a fiery Bride, opposing Antichrist and his forces with boldness and confidence, and having unprecedented authority. The boldness, confidence and authority will be a result of prayer and intimacy with Jesus.

The Bride's Destiny – Authority in Love

The desire of Jesus' heart is to see His Bride come forth at the end of the age loving and trusting Him totally, leaning upon Him (Song 8:5). In order for this to happen, we must aggressively depend on Him now and enter into abandonment to Him at the highest level. We must whole-heartedly accept His agenda and leadership. To abandon ourselves to Jesus, we must voluntarily embrace weakness. He wants us to wholly trust Him for all of our provision, wisdom, desires and sanctification (1 Cor. 1:30-31). Our destiny is to find our glory in Him alone, not in our giftings, strengths or riches (Jer. 9:23; 1 Cor. 1:31; Phil. 3:3). When she is mature, the Church will no longer have any confidence in or ties to the things of the world, but will have total confidence in Jesus and the things of God.

We are by nature full of pride, which moves us to assert ourselves and operate in a spirit of independence. In His mercy and lovingkindness, God removes our pride by His shaking and chastisement. He moves with jealous zeal to eliminate our desire to find comfort and contentment according to our own wills. He knows our sinful natures cause us to despise weakness and lean on anything and anyone other than God to find comfort when we are distressed. Even in times of prosperity and blessing, we often give up our dependency on God. We become intoxicated with our own importance and gratified by our own achievements and we are thus easily knocked off course.

In His kindness and as a protective mechanism, God is currently withholding the awesome power He will give His Church in the End-Times. He will restrain until He has dealt with our pride and prepared us to properly exercise the power we will receive. We will not be "earning" blessing and anointing as we submit to Him in obedience, but rather allowing Him to equip us to manage our coming authority. Authentic humility developed in us by God through grace, will position us to walk in true authority. Authentic humility rightly exalts Jesus at all times, in blessing and in trial. As we come together in corporate prayer and worship, we will be forced to deal with one another and face our hidden wrong attitudes and pride. As we do, we will develop meekness, and meekness will be the dominant characteristic of the coming victorious Church.

Only when our eyes are off ourselves and on Jesus, will we enjoy a love for Him that is authentic and mature. The Church will call Jesus her Beloved because she will be burning with unquenchable, unmovable and unshakable love for Him. This love will not quit or fail in the face of even the greatest pressure. The lovesick Bride will not be undone by religious attitudes of shame, fear and guilt.

Psalm 36:8-9 promises that the end-time Church will thrive in her love for Jesus, as she drinks from the river of His pleasures, and is abundantly satisfied with the fullness of His house. In other words, all of the supernatural reality of the heavenly realm itself will be available to come alive in the inner man of every believer in a whole new way in that time. God will provide, according to Ephesians 3:16, supernatural might on the inner man for those who ask Him for it. It is the increase by grace and the power of the Holy Spirit of the deep inner fire of love for God in the hearts of men and women. David described this as an enjoyable "river of pleasure" (Psalm 36:8), picturing a heart that flows like a river with tenderness and deep inner joy and satisfaction. It is significant that this Psalm was written by David as he faced an enemy more wicked than any man before him had. God has one answer for believers facing an evil foe: cultivate hearts and minds alive in love and satisfied by Jesus alone. Such hearts will be unfazed by earthly pressures, even those brought by Antichrist. Having intimacy with Jesus will empower the Church to serve and rejoice amid the outpouring of God's great wrath (Ps. 2:11-12).

Those who have spent their lives sowing in prayer and cultivating intimacy with Jesus will reap great rewards (Gal. 6:7). The Bride will begin to walk in more authority in prayer. While individuals have touched such dimensions of authority in prayer, the corporate Church has never operated in the level of power and authority in which she will operate at that time. It will be the type of authority that moves angels and demons, shifts the heavenly realms, and brings entire governments into the will of God. When the Church is walking in humility and meekness, and operating in power and authority, God will move forward.

A Change in the Expression of Christianity

God will bring massive transformation to Earth. He will fundamentally change the expression of Christianity. The Church is not taken seriously right now, but God will restore the Church to her rightful place. He will express Himself through His Bride in a way that will cause the nations to tremble. We know from Acts 5:11-14 that the early Church operated in signs and wonders. "So great fear came upon all the church and upon all who heard these things. And through the hands of the apostles many signs and wonders were done among the people. And they were all in one accord in Solomon's Porch. Yet none of the rest dared join them, but the people esteemed them highly. And believers were increasingly added to the Lord, multitudes of both men and women..."

This kind of response to the Church will come again. The victorious Church will be a conduit of heavenly power that moves the nations. In the process, people will take notice and consider the anointing on the Church. The radical lifestyles of believers will challenge the world's value systems and mindsets. Others will begin to wonder if Christianity really is the better way to live. They will begin to wonder if the Bible really might be true. As they consider these possibilities, they will begin to wonder what it all means for them.

The expression of Christianity will also change in terms of the Church's corporate lifestyle. As believers come into unity and operate in power and authority, people will be unsure how to relate to an entity with so much power. As judgments are released by the Church under the leadership of Jesus, people will begin to take the Church seriously again. The Bride's authority will engender esteem, trembling and godly fear from many. It will provoke anger, rage and contempt from others. Whatever their response, people will cease to be lukewarm towards the Church when judgment is released. They will be either for or against her, and therefore for or against God.

As the worldwide prayer movement matures, the Lord also will release anointing on His people to do the "greater works" promised by Jesus in John 14:12-14. Moses initiated and halted plagues according to his God-given authority. Elijah and Elisha parted waters, healed waters, raised the dead, out-maneuvered and defeated massive armies, initiated long droughts, multiplied food (2 Kin. 4:42-44), called down fire from heaven and slew evil prophets. The apostles moved in signs and wonders with "great power" (Acts 4:33) as a witness to the resurrection of the Lord Jesus.

The Church's anointing and power, however, will exceed that of any period in history. This massive increase will be necessary to counter the deception of the Antichrist and the False Prophet. Antichrist will deceive many with "all power, signs, and lying wonders" (2 Thess. 2:9). The False Prophet will perform "great signs," including calling fire down from heaven, to deceive people and bring glory to Satan (Rev. 13:13-14). But the Church in that hour will have been given an expression of the power of the Holy Spirit, which is superior to all other powers. The Church's power will far exceed in glory and might the power of Antichrist and the False Prophet. God's power will be unmatchable, just as in the days of Moses, when Pharaoh's magicians were eventually unable to match His power (Ex. 8:18-19). Throughout the world, a victorious Church will reap a great harvest of souls for Jesus by demonstrating true power (Rev. 14:14-15).

God will also send what the Bible calls "two witnesses" to lead the Church. He will give them incredible, unprecedented power, and they will oppose Antichrist in Jerusalem (Rev. 11). These two "anointed ones" were prophesied of thousands of years ago (Zech. 4:1-14). John described their ministry as a combination of Moses and Elijah. They will initiate plagues and call down fire from heaven. They will stop the rains and turn water into blood. They will be able to perform signs and wonders "as often as they desire" (Rev. 11:6). No one will be able to harm them for three and a half years.

The two witnesses are a picture of the anointing that will be upon the entire Body of Christ in that time. While the rest of the Church will not operate in power to the degree that the witnesses do, believers will have a more powerful anointing than ever before and will bear witness to the nations about the coming Kingdom of God. The huge measure of power given to the witnesses will be directly proportionate to their assignment from Heaven and their geographic location. They will oppose Antichrist in the Jerusalem temple. They will declare the "gospel of the kingdom," the pronouncement of the coming of the true King to Earth. There will be other "witnesses," or prophetic messengers and preachers of truth, preaching this gospel throughout the world to every nation (Matt. 24:14). Many are being called by God in this hour to prepare to proclaim the "gospel of the kingdom as a witness to all nations" (Matt. 24:14).

The stage for all of this will have been set when Jesus received the scroll, the "title deed" to Earth. Satan will have had control of the Earth until this time. When Jesus takes the scroll, it will signify the nearness of His Second Coming. As the rightful owner of Earth, He will return and claim what is His. He will take possession of His territory.

The prayers of the saints will have filled the bowls (Rev. 5:8) and the Church will be ready for Jesus to proceed. Neither He nor the Father will begin the final phase prematurely. If they were to initiate the Great Tribulation too early, many would be lost. Once Jesus has the scroll, He will open it, and as He does, He will break the seven seals on the outside of it. His breaking these seven seals will initiate the events that shake Earth and pave the way for Jesus to return.

ENDTIMES
simplified:

CHAPTER NINE:

The End of the Long Night

Once Jesus has received the scroll from the Father (Rev. 5), the first thing He will do is give the nations what they truly desire. According to Psalm 2:1-3, the coalition of nations will have fought to have its own way and its own king. The nations will rage against God and reject Him. They will desire their own rule of law, one with no biblical morality. When they reject God, He will give them over to their selfish desires.

It has always been the way of God to give people over to their desires, whether those desires are good and godly or bad and ungodly. This works for our good when we "ask, seek and knock" in pursuit of knowing Jesus. He will give us more of Him. But if we seek and choose to reject Him and His ways, He also will give us what we want: He will give us over to ourselves and let us go our own way. It is a principle of God that His judgment is to "give them up" to the lust of their hearts (Rom. 1:24). Those who persist in pursuing darkness will be eventually "given over" to their debased minds (Rom. 1:28). The frightening aspect of this principle is that ultimately, if people persist in their rebellion, God will "give them up" to the everlasting fire. If their deepest desire is to be separated from Him, God will allow them to be separated from Him for all eternity.

This principle will hold true in the End-Times as well. In the same manner God gives all of us over to our desires, whether good or evil, He will give the nations over to their desire to be without Him. God's wrath at this time will be global and terrible. As the nations exercise their freedom to do what is in their hearts, Earth will experience horrific chaos and upset. As God removes all restraint on a global scale, people will finally have permission to establish the evil laws that seem logical and right to their carnal minds. This will be the practical expression of the "fullness of the transgressors" described in Daniel 8:23.

The first thing the nations will receive from Heaven, as a result of God giving them over to their own desires, will be Satan himself. Satan will be cast down to Earth and he will be full of rage. The second thing the nations will receive will be the king they have wanted. This king will be Antichrist, the "man of sin" (2 Thess. 2:3).

This situation will be similar to what happened in Israel thousands of years ago. The nation of Israel was ruled by the King in Heaven, but in a blatant rejection of God, the Israelites petitioned the prophet Samuel for an earthly king. They asked for a king to govern them "like all the nations" (1 Sam. 8:5). In His kindness, God sent Samuel to the Israelites with a warning, because He wanted to change their hearts and convince them to stop asking for an earthly king "like all the nations." God had His own man in mind, King David, whom He was grooming to be a great, wise, just and kind king. God had already selected David as the king to establish His government around a tabernacle filled with singers and musicians praying and worshiping God night and day. God wanted to show the nations a different way to do government.

Despite God's warning, Israel persisted in asking for an earthly king according to their own timing, rather than trusting God and His timing. So God "gave them up" to their own desires, and gave them King Saul. And Saul was indeed just like every other king on Earth.

He was insecure, jealous, murderous and stubbornly independent. He saw God only as a means through which he could establish his own power base. Saul ended up insane and demonized. God had given Israel that for which she had asked, a king like the kings of all the other nations, but King Saul was hardly a blessing to them. He was a prototype for the Antichrist.

Jesus Breaks the Seven Seals

God will once again give the nations of Earth over to their evil desires and allow Antichrist to be their king. Antichrist will go forth "conquering and to conquer" (Rev. 6:2) as the result of Jesus breaking the first seal on the scroll He receives from the Father. At the breaking of the first seal, God also will grant permission for Jesus to move ahead, and in doing so, release fearsome judgment on the world. The nations will be given Antichrist as the king they wanted, and he will then conquer Earth.

The rise of Antichrist will also be the result of his declaring himself to be God and placing his image in the Jerusalem Temple. As the first seal is broken, Antichrist will demand that all people worship him as God and then enforce his command. His enforcement will be at first a bloodless conquest (Rev. 6:2), but will soon become a full-scale global war. When Jesus breaks the second seal, the false peace Earth will have known for three and one half years will be suddenly and viciously snatched away. When Jesus breaks the third seal, the world war waged by Antichrist will lead to a global famine. When Jesus breaks the fourth seal, one-fourth of all the people on Earth will die as a result of sword, hunger, disease and wild animals. It is important to note that the early phases of God's judgment on the nations will serve to demonstrate the true potential of men and women to cause their fellow human beings trauma, pain and suffering. It will shatter the illusions so many people have today that humanity is basically good and has the potential to accomplish good things apart from God.

The Church will be swept into this dramatic shift in global

climate. Many will be martyred as the rage of Satan is expressed through men and women. He will initiate his genocide of Christians and Jews, and as he does, will seal his own doom. For the prayer movement God has been cultivating for thousands of years will be mature (Rev. 5:8). As the judgments break out and Satan orchestrates the worldwide murder of the saints, God's underground prayer movement will burst forth in response, with higher levels of prayer than ever before. Not only will increased martyrdom fuel an increase in prayer, it will propel the prayer movement and the Church into a whole new realm of authority and power. The Church will participate via intercessory prayer in the Lord's release of judgments on Earth. As she does, she will become the chief foe of Antichrist, and the focus of his hatred. Then the fifth seal will be opened.

The breaking of the fifth seal will be more terrifying than the first four because of what it will awaken in Heaven and on Earth. This seal will loose a judgment more fierce and terrifying to unbelievers than the first four. God's prayer movement will evoke the fierceness of God's wrath against those martyring the saints, and His judgment will bring torment and death to those who oppose God. The Church will have a Psalm 149 authority in prayer for judgment. This authority, as in the case of the two witnesses, will release God's fire from Heaven (Rev. 8:3-4). The people of Earth will tremble at the prayers of the saints as the result. As promised in Luke 18:7-8, God will bring speedy judgment on those who persecute the saints to vindicate His reputation and His people.

Revelation 6:9-10 describes the golden altar of incense in Heaven, under which reside the believers slain because they would not back down from their testimony. The saints' intercession will arise to the throne, as they cry, "How long, O Lord, holy and true, until you judge and avenge our blood on those who dwell on the earth?" Their intercession will stir the heart of God to act in a new and more direct way in His wrath towards unrighteous and ungodly people. Up to this point, His judgments will have been fierce but indirect. He will have allowed people the freedom to devour one another in their rage. Now, God will be stirred with zeal for His beloved people and will move in a direct and fearsome way against the kingdom of Antichrist and all who stand with him. With the breaking of the sixth seal, He will bring extraordinary cosmic disturbances. The sky will roll back like a scroll and every land formation will be shifted.

Then Jesus will break the seventh and final seal, the most powerful of all the seals, which will initiate the sounding of seven trumpets (Rev. 8:2). Seven angels standing before God will each be commissioned, properly positioned, and given one of the seven trumpets. There will then be a chilling but glorious silence in Heaven, as all present anticipate the coming full release of God's judgments. The angels will be overwhelmed as all of Heaven awaits God's initiation of the climactic events that will end this age. The sudden silence in Heaven will be all the more chilling when juxtaposed against the horrifying sounds accompanying the breaking of the seals. As the seals were broken, John described hearing voices like thunder, intercessory cries, and cries of terror from the kings of Earth. But during the ensuing half-hour-long silence, he wrote that he heard absolutely nothing. The significance and dread of that silence is hard for us to even imagine.

The Sounding of the Seven Trumpets

The sounding of the seven trumpets and the judgments they usher In, wIll be both In response to and a reflection of the prayers of the saints. They will bring a mixture of mercy and vindication. The saints will have prayed for God to release judgment on their persecutors, but also that people would still repent. The trumpet judgments thus will serve three purposes. They will bring judgment on the enemies of the saints; warning to the lost that Jesus' arrival is imminent; and victory to God's people. The saints' victory will come as a result of true spiritual warfare, with all its elements of suffering, intercession, meekness and service (2 Cor. 10-12). The saints will not fight in a direct way, but in the patient manner of asking God to fight for them from Heaven.

The judgments that accompany the sounding of the seven trumpets will be akin to those of the Moses plagues. They will increase in intensity and culminate, when the sixth and seventh trumpets are sounded, in a shocking number of deaths. Moses was an earthly partner of God, and actively proclaimed, released and stopped the plagues through preaching and intercession. In the same manner, the saints will move in unity with the Lord to release judgment on the wicked in the hope that they will repent.

The first four trumpets will be used by God to destroy the provision, safety, and natural resources of Antichrist's worshippers (Rev. 8:7-12). Like the first four seals, these judgments will have an indirect effect on men. However, the last three trumpets, which the Bible calls "woes," will touch men in the Antichrist kingdom directly, using demons to torment and then kill them. The activity of the demonic realm will increase in intensity. The partial nature of the trumpet judgments will give those on Earth the opportunity to repent. The full cup of God's wrath, about which the angel spoke in Revelation 14:9-12, will culminate with God casting all who have rejected Him into the eternal lake of fire. Until the very end, however, God will provide opportunity for repentance. It will always be God's desire that none perish. Second Timothy 2:4 reminds us of God's desire that all men be saved and come to the knowledge of the truth. Those who realize the events are judgments from God, will tremble in fear and turn from wickedness.

We must always keep in mind that the severe judgments described in Revelation will not be brought because God has an angry attitude towards mankind. God loves every person He ever created, but will be deeply grieved by the nations' rejection and hatred of Him. The severity of His judgments will be proportionate to the hardness of people's hearts. We who have understanding of God's ways will never have cause to say He is too severe. We will understand His perspective and fully agree with His methods and leadership.

God has always and will always use the least severe means to produce the greatest amounts of love and repentance in human beings. Throughout history, God has moved in ways we may think extreme. But from a heavenly perspective, He has always done only what is absolutely necessary to deliver souls from the eternal lake of fire. When the time has come for the trumpets to sound, God will make one final attempt to get the attention of the nations before they harden their hearts completely towards Him. Once the nations fully reject God and declare war on Jesus upon His return to Earth, it will be too late for most. The level of deception will be so high by then, that many will actually view Jesus in His revealed glory as Satan himself. They will mourn, not rejoice, at His coming. So, in His mercy, God will be committed to saving as many souls as possible before the final moments come and there is no turning back.

The trumpet judgments will prove Antichrist's false gods to be inferior in power to Jesus. The supernatural acts of God will bring into submission to Jesus' jurisdiction both nature and demons. God will frustrate Antichrist's worldwide economic controls by striking down his natural resources. The trumpet judgments will be supernatural in nature and origin, in contrast to those of the first four seals, which were brought about by the unrestrained actions of sinful men and women.

Believers will not be the objects of the trumpet judgments, which God will hold back until the saints are sealed (Rev. 7:1-4). In his vision, John was told by the angel that the saints would be sealed before God struck the earth, sea and trees (Rev. 7:1-4), the areas devastated by the first four trumpet judgments (Rev. 8:7-11). Many believers will be protected during the end-time judgments (Zeph. 2:3; Mic. 7:14-19; Is. 11:15-16). While unbelievers are overcome by fear, the Church will be filled with faith (Luke 21:26-27). This dynamic contrast between the two groups will cause many people to take note of the Church's unshakable nature and come to salvation during what the Bible calls the Great Harvest.

The sounding of the last three trumpets will initiate the worst of God's judgments and be His final attempt to reach and save wicked people. In his vision, John saw an angel in heaven declaring with a loud voice, "Woe, woe, woe to the inhabitants of the earth, because of the remaining blasts of the trumpet of the three angels who are about to sound!" (Rev. 8:13). When the last three trumpets sound, Jesus' return to Earth will be near and He will soon declare war on darkness, and violently remove all who oppose Him. A multitude of people will be in the valley of decision (Joel 3:14), but time will be running out. The wicked nations will gather shortly thereafter in a literal valley in Israel and stage their last, desperate assault on Jesus. By the time they gather in the valley called Jehoshaphat, all final decisions will have been made, both theirs and God's. They will have decided to make war against His Son, and the Father will have decided to pour out the full measure of His wrath in final judgment that will come through the pouring out of the bowls, which will follow the trumpet judgments. The "woes" loosed when the last three trumpets sound will be God's final three trumpets. Revelation 9:21 says the wicked will not repent even then and their eternal destiny of damnation will be sealed.

The severity of the judgments brought forth by the sounding of the fifth and sixth trumpets is almost too shocking and terrifying to contemplate. Though severe, they will still be an expression of God's mercy to people on the brink of destruction. They will release demonic forces, which will be given permission by God to torment and then kill wicked people. These demons will be the same ones ungodly people will have worshiped (Rev. 9:21). Through the release of demonic forces, God will allow people to see for the first time the true nature of the demons they have openly worshiped. The first wave of demons will come from the abyss and be led by a demonic king named "Destroyer" (Rev. 9:11). These demons will torture the wicked for five months. The second wave will be led by four demonic captains who have "been prepared for the hour and day and month and year" (Rev. 9:15). They will be given permission by God to kill a third of mankind, and will lead two hundred million demons in this slaughter of the unrighteous.

The fate of the rebellious nations thus will be tragic. Though the wicked experience horrific consequences to their choices, they will not stop worshipping demons (Rev. 9:20-21). They will not repent of murder, sorcery, sexual immorality or theft. Combined with the actions of a demonic world dictator, devastating the Earth with his twisted policies, will be this unprecedented demonic activity. Immense suffering, grief, fear and rage will be rampant. People all over the world will be bitter at God, will betray their families and friends, and will be filled with hatred and deception. Occult practices and open worship of demons will increase in the midst of global famine and hardship. As people starve to death, their rage towards God will compel them to turn to these demons for "help." These same demons will betray, torment and ultimately kill them, but even as they suffer at the hands of the demons, they will remain loyal to them and continue to defy God. Because of their loyalty to spiritual darkness, Jesus will release literal darkness after the fourth trumpet sounds (Rev. 9:12). In that time, the day will end at noon (Amos 8:9), as God darkens the Earth in broad daylight.

Revelation 11:7-10 describes what will happen next. The two witnesses will be killed by Antichrist. Their dead bodies will lay in the streets of Jerusalem, which will have become an evil city, the likes of Sodom or ancient Egypt. No one will allow their bodies to be buried, and "those from the peoples, tribes, tongues, and nations" (Rev. 11:9), wicked people from all over, will come to rejoice over their deaths. The wicked will celebrate their deaths for three and one half days, "making merry" and sending gifts to one another (Rev. 11:10). They will believe the deaths of the two witnesses signify victory over God and the end of His tormenting judgments.

As the wicked celebrate, however, the two witnesses will be suddenly resurrected right before their eyes. After the three-and-one-half-day period, "the breath of life from God" will enter the witnesses and they will stand to their feet (Rev. 11:11). As the wicked tremble with fear at this turn of events and the witnesses rise, they will all hear the audible voice of the Lord telling the witnesses to "Come up here," and the witnesses will ascend to Heaven in a cloud

(Rev. 11:12). All will realize that not only has God not been defeated, but the judgments are not over. As the two witnesses ascend to heaven and their enemies watch in horror, Jesus will prepare to sound the seventh trumpet and proclaim the Kingdom of God. His return will be just around the corner.

At the sounding of the last trumpet, Heaven will break into great rejoicing, and proclaim, "The kingdoms of this world have become the kingdoms of our Lord and of His Christ, and He shall reign forever and ever!" (Rev. 11:15). John describes hearing loud voices shout this proclamation long-awaited by those in the courts of Heaven. Before He returns, however, Jesus will gather His saints to Himself in the sky.

The gathering of the saints in the sky has been called "the Rapture" of believers. Some suppose the Rapture and the Second Coming are the same event, while others believe they are separate events, which occur many years apart. Many who hold to the theory that they are separate events, believe the Rapture will take place before the Second Coming and before the Great Tribulation. However, a close reading of the Bible indicates that the Rapture will take place when Jesus bursts through the sky *after* the tribulation, which will last for 1,260 days. Other Scripture references to the tribulation state that it will be a period of 42 months or "time, times, and half a time," which equal one year, two years, and half a year (Dan. 7:25; 12:7; Rev. 11:2-3; 12:6; 13:5; 14). The abomination of desolation, or image of Antichrist, will remain in the temple for thirty more days after Jesus appears, according to Daniel 12:11. There will be a thirty-day period between Jesus' appearance in the sky and His defeat of Antichrist on Earth. This "appearing" in the sky will be but the first phase of Jesus' return to Earth, the opening moments of a return that will culminate in His triumph over Antichrist and his armies.

The Second Coming of Jesus

With the Kingdom proclaimed and the saints gathered unto

Jesus, one of the most incredible events in history will soon take place: the Second Coming of Jesus Christ. Since the creation of the world, Jesus has longed and waited for this moment. Thousands of years of labor will come to fruition in that moment, and all of Heaven will share in His almost uncontainable excitement. He will finally take what is His, all the nations of Earth. It will finally be time for Him to leave Heaven, gather His saints, and rescue His chosen people, the Jews. Paul said in 1 Thessalonians 4:16 that Jesus will go forth with a great shout, and the voice of an archangel will signal His battle cry. Vengeance for His enemies will be in His heart, and in righteousness He will judge and make war on them (Rev. 19:11). The nations will encounter the "winepress" of the fierceness and wrath of the Almighty God (Rev. 19:15). The Second Coming will take place just days after Jesus gathers His saints in the sky.

To properly understand the dynamics of the Second Coming, we must have the proper perspective. As Gentile believers, we focus on worshipping Jesus as God in the supernatural conditions of Heaven. We emphasize Jesus' deity as the Son of God. The Jews, however, have always thought of the Messiah as being an earthly King with whom they would reign in the natural conditions of Earth. They have always emphasized Messiah's humanity as the Son of David. The reality of Jesus, the Messiah, is that He is fully God and fully Man. The processes of the natural realm will not be suspended when He returns, but there will be a supernatural dimension to them. God created the physical, material Earth to be our home. But Earth will be profoundly impacted and enhanced by the supernatural as the two realms join together. As fully God and fully Man, Jesus provided a picture of the relationship between the natural and supernatural realms when He appeared in His resurrected body. Isaiah depicted this reality throughout his writing, describing dry and barren earthly deserts that suddenly bloom with glorious life. He described the beauty of Carmel and Sharon growing miraculously in the wastelands as parched ground became lush with springs of water (Is. 35:1-6).

Jesus described His appearance with some detail in two places, Matthew 24:29-31 and Luke 21:27-28. All the nations will see the sign of the coming of the "Son of Man," which is the Old Testament title of Messiah, the Deliverer of Israel. They will see Him in all of His glory with all of His angels when He breaks through the literal darkness. When the people of Earth who oppose Him see this, they will mourn deeply. The One whose purpose in coming to Earth is to make war against them, will be before them and only then will they realize the vastness of His power. His revealed glory will cause them to tremble in fright.

In Luke 21:28, Jesus said when the Church sees this event unfolding they should lift up their heads to the sky, for their "redemption draws near." The moment for which all believers have longed will have arrived. Jesus' procession in the sky, which may begin over Jerusalem with the rapture of the two witnesses, will then circumnavigate the world. It will not be possible for everyone to see Jesus at the same time. The global procession will last for days as Jesus sends His angels "with the sound of a great trumpet" (Matt. 24:31) to gather His elect from the four corners of Earth, from one end of the sky to the other. Many assume that this will be an "instantaneous" event, but Paul said in 1 Corinthians 15:52 that we will be *transformed* in a moment into our resurrected bodies. He did not say that we will be "caught up" in a moment. This is a process that will take time as "every eye will see Him" at His coming (Matt. 24:30). As believers look to the heavens, awaiting their angelic escort, all who have died in Christ will be raised incorruptible (1 Cor. 15:52). They will ascend to the sky first, and those alive when Jesus returns will be right behind them (1 Thess. 4:16-17), and will meet Jesus in the air. As believers are "caught up" into the air, they will be transformed "in the twinkling of an eye" (1 Cor. 15:52). In one moment, each believer's natural body will be transformed into what Paul calls a "spiritual body" (1 Cor. 15:44). Our spiritual bodies will be glorified physical bodies, like the physical body Jesus has possessed since His resurrection.

When the Israelites made their exodus from Egypt in the days of Moses, Pharaoh pursued them in order to kill and recapture his former slaves (Ex. 14). They were trapped between the Red Sea and Pharaoh and his army. The Israelites were terrified and defeat seemed inevitable. Both Israel and the Church will be in a similar position just before Jesus returns, as the forces of Antichrist close in. Before the Rapture, the situation will appear hopeless for Israel and for the Church. The Church will be confident because she will know the return of Jesus is near, but Israel will be terrified once more as all the nations surround Jerusalem (Zech. 12:2-3). Instead of parting the Red Sea, Jesus will split the sky and rapture the Church. Nearly thirty days after He comes to Earth to save those trapped in Jerusalem, Jesus will split the Mount of Olives in two (Zech. 14:4). Just as Pharaoh's army was drowned in the Red Sea, Antichrist's armies will be drowned in the "sea" of Jesus' bowls of wrath. In the next chapter, we will look at why there will be thirty days between when Jesus comes to Earth and when He rescues the Jews, and what will happen in that thirty-day period.

Isaiah gave a graphic picture of Jesus marching towards Jerusalem from Edom (Is. 63:1-6). He will come to rescue Jerusalem from the armies of the world. In that time, not one of the kings of Earth will align himself with Jesus. Jesus will be alone, but glorious in His apparel and mighty in strength. The One who is mighty to save will approach His battle with Antichrist with all power and strength, and knowing He will prevail. After His feet land on Mt. Sinai, Jesus will travel to Egypt, and there begin to release the bowls of wrath. There is a dual reason for Jesus to travel to Egypt to release these bowls of wrath or these supernatural signs of the power of God as He pours out His final expression of wrath among the rebellious nations of the world (Rev. 14:10).

The first reason involves Moses' prophecy about Jesus in Deuteronomy 18:15, where he said, "The LORD your God will raise up for you a Prophet like me from your midst, from your brethren." Jesus will be like a "second Moses," standing against an end-time

Pharaoh for the final deliverance of the Jewish people. Like Moses, Jesus will release terrible judgments that will secure this great deliverance. The bowls of wrath will cripple Antichrist's kingdom and force a desperate last stand against Jesus. The second reason Jesus will travel to Egypt, which will be discussed more in the next chapter, involves Jewish captives there who will be set free by Him (Is. 27:12-13).

As the forces of good and evil gather in a valley and surround Jerusalem to destroy her, human history as we know it will be drawing to a close. Jesus will have left Egypt and traced the exact path of Moses towards Israel. The nations will steel themselves, terrified but filled with rage, for one reason. Jesus will be in the land of Israel marching directly towards these armies. The long night will come to an end. A new day will be about to begin.

END-TIMES
simplified:

CHAPTER TEN

The Dawning of a New Day

In the final recorded vision of his life, Daniel learned the ultimate fate of his people, the Israelites, from an angel. Chapter Twelve of Daniel describes the climactic conclusion to Daniel's twenty-five-year journey of angelic visitations and end-of-the-age visions. As a young man, he had wrestled with theological issues involving God's chosen people, the Israelites, and their Babylonian captivity. The answers he received after a forty-year period of daily prayer and fasting are some of the most significant in the Word of God. Daniel wondered what would become of his people during and after their captivity. The angelic messengers of the Lord, including the angel Gabriel, revealed to Daniel much more than Israel's near future. The visions he received caused him physical pain, because he was distressed over the trauma his people would experience in the distant future. Despite the awful things his people would endure, however, Daniel received the revelation that the time of trouble "such as never was since there was a nation, even to that time" (Dan. 12:1), would also be the hour of ultimate deliverance for his people.

The angel described to Daniel the hour in which the saints

would rise from the dead, some receiving glorified bodies that will "shine like the brightness of the firmament," and others, who have turned many to righteousness, receiving bodies that will shine "like the stars forever and ever" (Dan. 12:3). Paul described this reward process in 1 Corinthians 15:35-49. The new bodies of the resurrected saints will shine to different degrees, like the celestial bodies (15:40-41). As each star differs from the next in glory, so it will be with the resurrected bodies of believers.

After the angel told him what would happen, Daniel had one question. One of two nearby angels asked the very question on Daniel's mind: "How long shall the fulfillment of these wonders be?" (Dan. 12:6). The original angel answered immediately, and told him there would be a three-and-one-half-year period of unprecedented trouble. Before the end of the age came, when "all these things shall be finished," the "power of the holy people would be completely shattered" (Dan. 12:7). Daniel had realized great trouble would come in the End-Times, and he had realized a demonized, powerful world dictator would oppress and kill the saints; but until he heard "completely shattered," he had not realized just how dreadful the situation at the end of the age would be for his people. When this realization set in, he wondered aloud if his people would survive. "My lord, what shall be the end of these things?" (Dan. 12:8).

This is the same question every believer wants answered. We all want to know how the story will end, and whether everyone will make it through safely. The angel's answer gave Daniel little comfort: "Go your way, Daniel, for the words are closed up and sealed until the time of the end." The angel was in essence telling Daniel that the answers he sought could not be given at that time. The angel did, however, offer a hint. Though the unprecedented time of trouble for the saints would be for three-and-one-half years, the abomination of desolation would remain for thirty days beyond that. What will happen during this thirty-day period? Why will there be thirty days in which the saints are not subjected to the great pressure and rage of the Antichrist, though he will still be in power, as seen by the abomination of desolation remaining in the temple? The answer that unfolds throughout Scripture is that Jesus will be on Earth, guiding events toward an epic battle, which will begin with the liberation of captive Jews and culminate with the liberation of captive Jerusalem.

The Battle of Jerusalem

Israel has experienced many terrible times during her long history, but the time just prior to Jesus' return will be the worst. None of Israel's past suffering will compare with what will take place then. There will be a second, world-wide Jewish holocaust, worse than the first. The Word of God has many references to prison camps and horrific conditions for the Jewish people before Jesus comes. Isaiah 42 is one such passage, in which the Lord promised that He would open blind eyes and rescue prisoners who sit in darkness in their death camps (42:7). When Jesus begins to restore the Earth, He will commence by calling out to the prisoners, "Go forth," and to those in darkness, "Show yourselves" (Is. 49:8-9). Psalm 102 was written "for the generation to come" (verse 18) from the perspective of a prisoner in a prison camp. The prisoner anticipates the hour in which God will look down from Heaven and "hear the groaning of the prisoner, to release those appointed to death."

As Jews and Christians around the world face the horrors of prison camps and other atrocities, the Jews living in Israel will also face a huge problem. The armies of the nations will conquer Israel and surround Jerusalem to destroy her. Zechariah depicts the events of that hour in Chapters 12-14. The scene will be terrifying. During that final siege, Jerusalem will be "like a cup of drunkenness to all the surrounding peoples" (Zech. 12:2). Zechariah goes on to say that two-thirds of the population of Israel, *millions* of Jews, will be slaughtered (Zech. 13:8). As the raiding armies continue to pummel the city, incited to a drunken rage in their demonic zeal, the remainder of the Jews will wait in terror to die. Zechariah 12:3 describes it as the time when every nation on Earth will have come to "heave away" this "heavy stone" called Jerusalem.

Jesus will be the cause of the nations' rage. His return will incite the armies to gather and lay siege to Jerusalem. All the nations will have seen Him appear as He made His way "from east to west" around the world (Matt. 24:27), and everywhere men and women will have mourned as He crossed the sky with His glorious procession. Some will mourn because they have heard about this moment for many years from believers and are now faced with the truth. Some will have taken the mark of the beast (Rev. 13:17; 14:9-11) and now have to face the consequence of that decision. Some will mourn because the Antichrist will have warned them about the coming of Jesus for years, and they believe they must now defeat the Man whom Antichrist will paint as the "false Messiah." None will be prepared for the sheer power, glory and majesty of Jesus. Jesus' breathtaking journey across the sky will cause even the most hardened and arrogant of His foes to tremble. As a result, most people in the world will be stirred by His coming and will gather to fight Him.

It is likely that His journey around the world will end at the most astonishing of places: Mount Sinai. From there Isaiah said that the Messiah (Jesus) would travel to Egypt and free Jewish captives there (Is. 11:11-16). It is also there that He will begin to release the bowls of wrath. He will next travel to Assyria to free Jewish captives and rescue those about to perish. Isaiah 27:12-13 describes this process: "In that day that the Lord will thresh, from the channel of the River to the Brook of Egypt; and you will be gathered one by one, O you children of Israel. So it will be in that day: the great trumpet will be blown; they will come, who are about to perish in the land of Assyria, and they who are outcasts in the land of Egypt, and shall worship the Lord in the holy mount at Jerusalem."

Zechariah 10:10 says the same thing: "I will also bring them back from the land of Egypt, and gather them from Assyria." It will be an awesome sight, as the Son of David, surrounded by the resurrected saints and an angelic host, marches towards Israel (Zech. 14:5).

The nations will be stunned at what Jesus accomplishes in His strength. He will continue liberating captives and releasing the terrible bowls of wrath, in concert with His Father in Heaven. The desire for self-preservation will grip even the "kings from the east" (Rev. 16:12), who will have resisted the Antichrist regime until their water supply turned to blood (Rev. 16:4). This will enable Antichrist to convince these nations to join him in resisting this new enemy who has emerged. Jesus in that hour will appear to be the greatest threat that mankind has ever faced.

When the first four bowls are released, all who have taken the mark and worshipped the image of Antichrist will be afflicted with a "foul and loathsome sore" (Rev. 16:2). Many afflicted with sores will be those who have persecuted the Church and murdered the Jews. The sores will represent a mark from God to remind them of their coming doom, and they will be gripped by fear and enraged. Next, the seas will turn to blood, the oceans of Earth will literally become blood "as of a dead man" (Rev. 16:3). The foul blood will kill every living creature of the sea, thus crippling Earth's food supply. People will be forced to drink blood to survive as "their just due" (Rev. 16:6). As they have been brutal and bloodthirsty in their lust to kill and destroy the saints and prophets of God, God's judgment on them will be to give them that for which they sought: blood.

Those in Jerusalem will probably hear about the Moses-like figure in Egypt who is releasing supernatural signs, and will wonder who He is and why He is coming to their rescue. Some may hear of the mighty works of His hand in freeing Jewish captives in the Egyptian and Assyrian regions; others may hear of the Moses-type signs and wonders that are erupting, fulfilling the promise of Micah 7:12-15: "As in the days when you came out of the land of Egypt, I will show them wonders." They may hear of His march from Bozrah to Jerusalem (Is. 63:1). With all of these scattered bits of information, there will appear to be much confusion regarding the true identity and nature of Jesus. The people of the world and the Jews will all ask, "Who is this King of Glory?" (Ps. 24:10). As Jesus comes to their aid by releasing bowls of wrath that cripple Antichrist's power base, the Jews will be shocked at His "Jewishness," at how alike them He is and how much He understands their national history. They will not realize yet that their history is actually His history and their destiny is in Him.

While the Jews will be perplexed because of the way in which this mysterious figure is fulfilling their well-known scriptural promises, they also will be hopeful. In contrast, the nations will be more enraged than ever. With their food supply lacking and the fresh waters of Earth filled with blood, the hardening of their hearts will come to completion. Paul described the root cause of the condition in which they will find themselves when he wrote, "They did not love the truth, that they might be saved" (2 Thess. 2:10). These people will have willfully "forgotten" about God because they didn't want to submit to Him and alter their lifestyles (2 Peter 3:5-7). Because they will have chosen to live according to their own agendas and to reject the truth of God, God, in His perfect justice, will give them their "just due" (Rev. 16:6).

Those who have rejected God's truth will hence come to the end of their journey into wickedness. There will be no love for God in them, and they will be totally hard-hearted. Indeed, they will be at the point of no return. They will blaspheme the Name of God during the judgments released by the next two bowls of God's wrath, scorching heat and terrifying darkness. By the release of the sixth bowl of wrath, as seen in Revelation 16:12-16, they will become fully reprobate. They will have, like the Egyptian Pharaoh many thousands of years before, become so hardened that God Himself will participate in the hardening of their hearts (Ex. 9:12; 10:20, 27). The release of the sixth bowl will be the moment in which millions around the world who have been offended or angry at God will come off their fence of indecision. They will join Antichrist in making war against Jesus (Rev. 19:20:19), having been deceived into thinking that Jesus is the evil one, bent on their destruction.

The release of the sixth bowl will be followed by a "strong

delusion" (2 Thess. 2:11-12) sent from Heaven to cause the hard-hearted to believe the lie that Jesus is an agent of the devil, or even the devil himself. The very definition of the blasphemy of the Holy Spirit, or the "unpardonable sin" (Matt. 12:32), is for people to be so hardened in heart and deceived in thinking that they call the loving actions of the Holy Spirit to be "of the devil," as the Pharisees did in Jesus' day. According to Revelation 16:13, the nations will be tricked by Satan into believing that Jesus is actually the Antichrist, dedicated to destroying the world, overthrowing the kings, and taking over rule. The sixth bowl will point towards a global blasphemy of the Holy Spirit and will be the point of no return for many in the world. There will be no more forgiveness after this point, which is why the sixth bowl will be the most terrifying judgment up to this point.

In other words, as Jesus releases the judgments of the sixth bowl, He also will allow the demonic deception of Satan to be released on those who now stand against Him. Thus, kings and leaders who had previously resisted Antichrist or openly opposed him, will change their minds. They will cross the newly dried up Euphrates River and join the other kings gathering there to make war against Jesus. The drying up of the river will serve as a false sign of the Antichrist's power to oppose Jesus, and all of these kings will believe in this false power. They will think that it is possible, if they join together with the power of Antichrist, to defeat this great threat marching towards them from Bozrah.

They will be enticed and energized by "spirits of demons, performing signs" (Rev. 16:14), and thus lead their armies to the gathering point, the Valley of Jehoshaphat, to attack Jerusalem. This staging area, also known as Mount Megiddo, has been widely recognized as the "crossroads of the nations." Three continents come together in this region of Northern Israel, giving it strategic value. Historically, those who have controlled this region have had a significant advantage in war. The armies will be led by a desperate Antichrist and his False Prophet, who will be set on completing their satanic plan to eliminate the people of promise.

As the armies converge, thousands of Jews will be trapped in Jerusalem. Having been completely broken as a people, their will to fight will be almost non-existent. Even with the mysterious Mighty King marching to save them, they will feel little hope. They will cry out and wail, and many will repent. When the situation seems utterly hopeless, however, something significant will suddenly happen. Jesus will release the seventh bowl, and the most powerful earthquake in history will strike Earth. Mountains will collapse and violent waters will cover the islands. Babylon, one of the most powerful cities in the world, will be totally destroyed, never to rise again. Mighty hailstones will fall upon the wicked armies and people will rage and cry out with their final blasphemies against God (Rev. 16:21). What began with the seventh trumpet in Heaven will be ended by the release of the seventh bowl.

Then Jesus will ride into battle on a white horse (Rev. 19:11), clothed in white and accompanied by the armies of Heaven. The fullness of God's wrath towards wickedness will be fully released through His Son on this "day of vengeance" (Is. 63:4). Jesus will effortlessly slaughter the armies of Earth as He enters into what Isaiah described as the "winepress of the nations" (Is. 63: 3-6). Many, many soldiers (Rev. 19:21) and world leaders (Ps. 110:5-6) will be slain in the final battle, when Jesus strikes the nations and executes the rebellious kings. Blood will flow out of the valley for 184 miles (Rev. 14:20), and will at some points be as high as the bridle of a horse. According to Isaiah, Jesus Himself will be completely covered in His enemies' blood. "All His robes" will be stained (Is. 63:3). John indicated the same in Revelation 19:13, when he said Jesus will be clothed in a robe "dipped in blood." By "dipped in blood," John didn't mean that just a corner of His robe will have blood on it; he meant Jesus will appear to be fully covered in blood.

Zechariah 14:1-7 gives more detail regarding what will happen at this climactic battle for Jerusalem. Because of the fifth bowl of utter darkness, it will literally be the darkest day in history. Amos 5:18-20 says this day will be a day that is "very dark, with no brightness in it." It will be a tense time for those trapped in the city. There will have been a great earthquake, hail, and the destruction of battle. The forces of Antichrist will be closing in, looking to finish them off. As when they were trapped between Pharaoh and the Red Sea, they will be trapped, this time in a city partially destroyed by the massive quake of the seventh bowl, up against the Mount of Olives, and desperate for their Deliverer to come. Suddenly, He will! The mountain behind them will part like the Red Sea thousands of years before when Jesus sets His foot upon it (Zech. 14:4).

Jesus thought about this moment two thousand years ago as He promised, "For assuredly I say to you, whoever says to *this* mountain, 'Be removed and cast into the sea,' and does not doubt in his heart..." (Mark 11:23). He was standing on the Mount of Olives when He made that statement. "This mountain," according to Zechariah, will split in two from east to west and make a large valley through which those trapped in Jerusalem can escape. "Thus the Lord my God will come," Zechariah said emphatically, "and all the saints with You." The Jews' flight to safety will enable Jesus to finish this great battle. "But in the evening time it shall happen that it will be light," Zechariah said in describing the end of the struggle that marks the end of this age. The light is a reference to the dawning of a new day. It shows the emergence of a glorious transition, the end of the kingdom of mankind and the birth of the Kingdom of God on Earth.

At the end of the battle, Antichrist and the False Prophet will be captured and cast alive into "the lake of fire burning with brimstone" (Rev. 19:20). Satan, the defeated prince of the world, will be captured as well, and chained up by an angel. He will be stripped of all authority and power, and his kingdom will be dismantled as the Kingdom of God overtakes Earth. God will set a seal on Satan as He casts him into the same pit from which "Legion" begged to be spared two thousand years earlier (Luke 8:30-32). Satan will be trapped in this prison and unable to deceive anyone for the thousand-year period of Jesus' reign on Earth.

Blessed is He Who Waits

In addition to the two groups discussed so far, the saints in the Church and the wicked who hate God, there is a third group of people who will be alive throughout the End-Times and after the final battle. This group will be comprised of people who are not saved Christians, but who refused to take the mark of the beast during the three-and-one-half-year period of trials. These people will be unsaved survivors who refused to worship Antichrist, but who were not converted in the Great Harvest at the end of the age. The Bible refers to this group as "the ones who are left" and "the ones who remain" (Is. 4:3; 10:20; 11:11; 49:6; 65:8; 66:19; Jer. 31:2; Ezek. 20:38-42; 36:36; Dan. 12:1; Amos 9:9-10; Joel 2:32; Zech. 12:14; 13:8; 14:16).

In studying the End-Times, many people don't know how to explain or understand the existence of this group of people. They wonder how or why an unsaved person could refuse the mark. The language of the Book of Revelation seems to indicate that all whose names are not written in the book of life will take the mark (Rev. 13:8). Further, the language in Revelation 13:16 seems to imply that all people will be forced to take it. On the other hand, Zechariah 12:10-14 describes Jesus interacting with "all the families that remain" in the land after the great battle. Those among the one-third of the Jewish population who survive the time of trouble will all come to salvation after the battle. None of them will have taken the mark. There are other passages, such as Psalm 48 and Revelation 21:24, which speak of Jesus interacting with earthly kings. It would not be possible that these kings were saved prior to the conflict; otherwise, they would have been raptured with the saints. Likewise, they couldn't have been among the wicked kings opposing Jesus, or they would have been killed. They must, therefore, belong to the third group, those not saved but not in opposition to God.

Additionally, Revelation 22:2 says the leaves of the tree of life "were for the healing of the nations" (Rev. 22:2). The nations will need healing after the final battle because this third group of people will remain on Earth with unresurrected bodies, and they will need healing. Many of the unsaved survivors will be converted and become believers as Jesus begins the process of rebuilding Earth.

It is not clear why this group of people will exist. It may be because their names were always written in the book of life in the foreknowledge of God. It may be God will have mercy on them, as He will have mercy on whomever He will have mercy (Rom. 9:15). What we can know for certain is that, while mortals will be as rare as fine gold after God's wrath has been poured out (Is. 13:12), there nonetheless will be some mortals. Isaiah 66:19 says Israel will declare the glory and the greatness of the Lord to all the Gentiles who survive, for the Lord will spare many for the sake of His servants (Is. 65:8). Ezekiel 36:36 says, "the nations which are left all around you shall know" that the Lord has rebuilt the ruined places in that day.

So there will be several groups of people who survive the final battle. One group will be the Jews who have survived all the trouble and trauma of the last days. As Jesus enters the city triumphantly, the Holy Spirit will pour out "the Spirit of grace and supplication" (Zech. 12:10) upon these Jews. The spirit of prayer will fill them and cause them to mourn deeply over their sins and their rejection of Jesus at His first coming. The entire land will mourn and grief will overwhelm them, unto deep repentance. The Jewish people will finally recognize Jesus as Messiah, and acknowledge the One they pierced (Zeph. 3:18; Zech. 12:10). The leaders and people of Jerusalem will receive Him and shout, "Blessed is He who comes in the name of the Lord!" This will fulfill the prophetic word spoken 2,000 years ago by Jesus to the spiritual leaders of Jerusalem (Matt. 23:39).

Jesus will commence the rebuilding process by opening a fountain in Jerusalem. This fountain will be a blessing and cleansing agent. Idolatry will be cut off there for all time. He will deal with false prophets and the unclean spirit, most likely Satan himself. As mentioned, Satan will be cast into the abyss. Jesus and the saints will oversee the process of rebuilding the devastated Earth, and the remaining population will assist them. The rebuilding process will take many years, but Jesus eventually will establish His Kingdom throughout the world. The nations will be trained in the ways of the Lord (Is. 2:1-4); the law will go forth out of Zion; and all those on Earth will be discipled by Jesus and the saints. New government systems will be established, and true global peace will exist.

The Feast of Tabernacles will be celebrated again soon after Jesus' monumental and glorious triumph, and people will celebrate deliverance from Satan and his wicked followers. The spiritual atmosphere of the world will begin to shift as prophetic songs fill the hearts of newly saved men and women and are heard while the ruined places are restored and rebuilt (Is. 61:1-4). "The Branch of the Lord shall be beautiful and glorious; and the fruit of the earth will be excellent and appealing for those of Israel who have escaped" (Is. 4:2). The Kingdom of Heaven, like a mustard seed, will start small but eventually become the resting place for the nations of Earth (Matt. 13:31).

Many other things will take place as Jesus reigns on Earth. Matthew 25:31-46 says Jesus will begin to set up thrones and gather the nations to judge them for their refusal to align themselves with Him at the battle of Jerusalem. All of those who are left on Earth will be judged and evaluated by Jesus, as He determines who of the unsaved survivors will enter the Kingdom. One determining factor will be how they treated God's "brethren" during the Great Tribulation. God's "brethren" refers to the now-saved remnant of Jews who survived the final battle, as well as the now-resurrected believers. Jesus also will build a great throne and rebuild a glorious new Temple in Jerusalem (Ezek. 40-48). As He does, something supernatural and glorious will take place that will unite His earthly throne with His heavenly throne. Heaven will become God's throne, and the Earth His footstool (Is. 66:1). Ezekiel 43:7 calls the earthly Temple "the place of My throne and the place of the soles of My feet, where I will dwell in the midst of the children of Israel forever." In speaking of the Millennial Temple as the footstool of His throne, Jesus was speaking of the New Jerusalem emerging from Heaven and dwelling over the earthly Jerusalem in the sky for a thousand years (Rev. 21:10).

The angel of Daniel 12 gave Daniel a hint about how this would come about. He indicated that though the abomination of desolation will be removed thirty days after Jesus raptures the Church, there will be an encouragement for those who "wait" until forty-five days after the Rapture. The angel told Daniel that those who wait will be "blessed." The angel then encouraged Daniel that he would arise, or be resurrected into his inheritance, at the end of the age. The question is, what is coming to those who will be blessed, and what will the inheritance be to which Daniel will arise? It is possible that the 45-day mark will signal the official end of this age and the breaking in of a significant portion of our inheritance from God. This may be when the New Jerusalem "descends out of heaven" (Rev. 19:10). John saw the New Jerusalem (Rev. 21:9-27), which is part of the inheritance for which the great heroes of the faith have been waiting, according to Hebrews 11. Hebrews 11:10 says Abraham waited for this city, understanding that it would be his true inheritance, not the actual land of Israel in his time. Hebrews 11:13-15 says those who died in faith were "awaiting a better homeland" or "a heavenly country," understanding that the city that God had prepared for them, the New Jerusalem, would be the heavenly home of all the saints.

The New Jerusalem will not, however, immediately settle onto Earth. It will be a glorious and massive "satellite city," which floats over the earthly Jerusalem for the one thousand years that Jesus reigns on Earth. Scripture gives us some information about the relationship between the New Jerusalem and the Earth during the thousand-year reign of Jesus. There will be a connection between

Earth and the heavenly city before it finally settles onto the New Earth. The connecting point for the two realms will be the throne of Jesus. His throne will connect the earthly Jerusalem, which will measure 10 square miles (Ezek. 48:30-35), with the heavenly New Jerusalem, which will measure 1,500 square miles (Rev. 21:16). Earth will be the "footstool" of the throne of Jesus as the two realms of Heaven and Earth connect but do not yet merge. The ancient throne of the king had two parts, the seat, or chair, and the footstool. One would not consider these parts two distinct thrones, but would view the two pieces as one throne. This is what the Isaiah 66:1 passage spoke of: two places (Heaven and Earth), but one throne for Jesus during His one-thousand-year reign over the nations. Jesus will live in the New Jerusalem, His throne will connect both the heavenly and earthly realities, and from this throne He will rule the nations.

The old Earth will not be able to contain this massive city, with its unfathomable dimensions, until it is fully restored by Jesus. Not only will the land have to be reformatted to contain this city in its width and depth, but the atmosphere itself will have to be reconfigured to extend further into space, much beyond our present breathable atmosphere, in order to contain the heights of the great New Jerusalem. In other words, a "new heavens" will have to be formed. There are deserts in Egypt that Isaiah said will burst into bloom during the reign of the Messiah (Is. 35:1-7) that would be crushed under this massive city were it to settle onto the Earth right away. Nations would be underneath this 1,500-mile-wide city, whose dimensions will stretch from the eastern coast of the United States to the Mississippi River. In the meantime, the throne of Jesus will bridge the heavenly city with Earth. The New Jerusalem will be home to the resurrected saints and God, until all the people on Earth are suitably prepared to relate to God face to face.

The New Jerusalem will serve and bless the nations during the thousand-year reign of Jesus in many ways. It will be our home, but also will contain the tree of life, whose leaves will bring "healing to the nations" (Rev. 22:2). The nations will flow to the "mountain house of the Lord" (Is. 2:2-4) and learn the anointed way to live and "the ways of God," that they might walk in His paths. It will be the starting point for the mighty River of God (Ezek. 47:1-12), which will flow from the throne (Rev. 22:1) and bring refreshing to the desert places of the world. It will bring light to the saved nations of the world (Rev. 21:24). Earth will need all 1,000 years of the millennial reign to be prepared to contain this city. When the time comes for the New Jerusalem to settle onto Earth, the nations will be healed and the people will be fully mature and fully given to God. They will no longer have any rebellion or hidden wrong attitudes.

The main goal of Jesus' thousand-year reign will be to prepare the nations for the coming of His Father to Earth. God has longed since the Fall to be fully with us again and Jesus has always been committed to making this a reality. He will labor with the saints to prepare every nation and people to be in deep, face-to-face intimacy with God for all eternity.

The end of the thousand-year preparation process will bring one final test for those remaining on Earth, those not raptured when Jesus returned (Rev. 20:7-10). Those who were unsaved when Jesus returned will have given birth to children throughout the thousand-year reign. The people of these later generations, those born during the millennial reign, will have been fully Christianized under the leadership of Jesus, but not all will be truly in love with God. There will be those who quietly resent Jesus' leadership. For example, Zechariah 14:16-21 indicates that the people of Egypt will refuse to come to Israel to celebrate the Feast of Tabernacles, resisting Jesus' summons to all the world to come and commemorate its deliverance.

It may seem odd that there will be those who sin during the millennium; at least until we remember how much sin exists in the Church today. The unfortunate and uncomfortable truth is that sin exists within the Body of Christ, in our own churches. Sincere believers who love Jesus struggle with sin now and believers will continue with that struggle until the end of the millennial reign.

While there will be sin during that time, there will be some difference between that time and our present condition. With Satan bound, the temptation to sin will be significantly diminished, and there will be much less opportunity for sin to be expressed. It will be much easier to obey the Lord than it is now. The problem is that it will also be easy to become complacent, but appear to be obedient. The hidden attitudes and frustration with the leadership of Jesus will have no context in which to be expressed. Choice is the greatest test of love, as well as the greatest gift God gives us to grow in love. We will always have the freedom to choose to love Him. In that day, the people on Earth during His millennial reign will have that same freedom, and will still wrestle with their sinful natures.

The nations of the world will be offered one final choice. One final option will be given to the nations as the Garden of Eden scenario plays out again at the end of the thousand-year reign of Jesus. The Lord Himself will orchestrate this, to test people's hearts to discover what is authentic and reveal what is hidden. Only that which is authentic love will be able to endure the full glory of the Lord that will cover Earth. Thus Satan will be released from his long imprisonment. He will deceive many in that time; the number will be as "the sand of the sea" (Rev. 20:8). This number will surprise many, but Jesus will not be surprised. He will perceive the true state of people's hearts. God's release of Satan to entice those who rebel against joining Him is for our benefit and theirs, not His. Those who hate God must and will be removed, because the result of their hatred would be further attempts to overthrow God and destroy the righteous. Their bitterness would only increase with the passage of time once their choices were made.

Once God swiftly and conclusively deals with the rebellious and wicked, Earth will enter its next phase of history. We cannot be sure of what that new age, which we call eternity, will look like for us, but we do know the Father has been waiting and planning for that time from before the creation of the world. Right now, Jesus is yearning and longing to return for His Bride. Right now, the Father is yearning and longing to be reunited fully with His precious children. Whatever the Father has in store for us in eternity, we can be certain it will be glorious and wonderful. Our destiny is to grow in our knowledge of His love for us and to grow in our love for Him, and grow in our capacity to know and receive His love, forever and ever.

END-TIMES
simplified:

EPILOGUE:

On the Other Side of Eternity

"Beloved, now we are children of God; and it has not yet been revealed what we shall be, but we know that when He is revealed, we shall be like Him, for we shall see Him as He is" (1 John 3:2). In this verse, John offered encouragement to his friends in the churches, for whom he had cared over the past few years. He encouraged them to live according to the promise and truth that abided in them, a living truth connected to the assurance of eternal life. He urged them to cut off their love for the things of the present world and their attachments to worthless, temporal things.

For us to be ones who abide forever with God, we must set our affections on the only thing that stands forever: the Word of God, which indicates what God's will is. We must receive the words of John in our hearts and decide to live for eternity, rather than for today only. The cry of John's heart when he authored 1 John was for people to understand that, as children of God, we are children of promise, children of eternity. He wanted us to grasp that the greatest expression of love we can offer to God is to obey Him with all of our hearts. The Father has bestowed His immense and perfect love upon us, a love so fantastic and otherworldly that, when properly understood and received, causes our hearts to soar with delight and sing with everlasting joy. Those who love God have the honorable distinction of being called "children of God."

Being children of God has implications so vast and wonderful and grand with regard to our destinies, we can hardly fathom them. Unfortunately, few people even try. Few people pause to consider the benefits that come as a result of holding the title "child of God." And those who do consider the benefits usually don't consider the full scope of them. While even the most basic of benefits, such as being happy, not shedding any more tears, and knowing true peace, are wonderful and worthy to be considered, they are almost nothing compared with the greatest of all benefits: living in perfect relationship with God for all eternity and being wed to His Son Jesus forevermore.

When Jesus returns, a perfected love will have been worked in every believer. The journey from where we are now to where we need to be is one of preparation. In order to lay hold of this perfected love, we must be willing to do whatever it takes to prepare for that encounter. The love of Jesus must be perfected in us *before* we finally encounter Him face to face. Jesus said He wants us to "be perfect as your Heavenly Father is perfect" (Matt. 5:48). The Amplified Bible translation of this verse describes the process of love being perfected in us as that of "growing into complete maturity of godliness in mind and character, having reached the proper height of virtue and integrity." As John the beloved disciple said in his first letter, our hope must involve more than salvation from Hell and escape from our present unpleasant circumstances. Our hope is related to what the future holds for us and is inseparably linked to faith and love. The height of hope is found in perfected love.

John also wrote in the same letter that the "blessed hope" to which Titus 2:13 refers, is about far more than even the glorious appearance of Jesus in the sky. While the blessed hope is partially about seeing the Son of Man appear with righteous vengeance to rescue the saints, vindicate His Father, and claim what is His, it is about even more. This hope has a deeper dimension. According to John, this hope is also about our eagerness to discover who we will be when we see Jesus "as He is" (1 John 3:2). We do not yet know what we will be like when our bodies are transformed into their resurrected, eternal, glorified states. Just as Jesus will be beautiful beyond measure, we will be amazed at our own revealed beauty and glory.

In his letter to the Philippians, Paul wrote that he was expending all his might and focus to the work of knowing Jesus fully, in every dimension that is possible to know Him, including joining in His suffering. The reason he gave was, "…if, by any means, I may attain to the resurrection from the dead" (Phil. 3:11). Paul understood eternal reward. He longed to receive the full measure of the reward that would come to Him at the resurrection. The reward we will each receive is one that will last for all eternity. In His sovereignty, God is orchestrating each of our lives with His big picture in mind. He knows what we shall be, but has not yet revealed it to us. The real and full dimension of who we really are cannot be known apart from our "real" lives, which will be revealed in the age to come. In the next age, the age to come, we will begin a whole new journey. We cannot know now what we will be doing a billion years from now, but we can be sure it will be magnificent and fantastic and beyond our wildest dreams.

God, of course, knows what we will be doing. He sees the end from the beginning and knows all the magnificent things He has planned for us. The Bible contains surprisingly little information about our life with God in eternity. There are hundreds of verses about the final years of this age and the Millennial Kingdom of Jesus, but there is not much in the Word of God about our destiny beyond that point. We do know a few facts from Scripture. We know there will be no end to the "the increase of His government and peace" (Is. 9:7). We know that from His throne, Jesus will order and establish His kingdom with judgment and justice "from that time forward, even forever" (Is. 9:7). We know Israel will inherit the land forever promised to Abraham, and will maintain possession of it throughout eternity. We know the sons of Levi will stand and minister in the name of the Lord forever.

We know also we will live forever in the New Jerusalem, which will come out of Heaven and settle onto the New Earth after Jesus' thousand-year reign. The New Jerusalem on the New Earth will be the literal inheritance of Israel and the saints forever, and the location of the throne of Jesus. The Father Himself will dwell with us there. We will relate face to face with the Father for the first time since Adam and Eve related to Him that way in the Garden of Eden. The Father Himself will be our "exceedingly great reward" for our labors now and in the Millennial Kingdom. We will spend all of eternity enjoying our "Great Reward." We will continue to grow forever in love for God and in our capacity to receive His love. We will be forever exploring the depth, the width, the length and the height of the great ocean of God's love for us.

While we can't know all the details of what our life will be like in eternity, we must realize that what we do now will directly impact who we will be and what we will do then. Our choices today really do have an eternal impact. As we follow His ways, obey His commands, and seek to love Him with all of our hearts, God will help us to know the "hope of His calling" and "the riches of the glory of His inheritance in the saints" (Eph. 1:18). God wants us to ask Him for "the spirit of wisdom and revelation in the knowledge of Him" (Eph. 1:17). God wants to give us prophetic insight into our eternal destiny. He wants to make mysteries known to us through the Holy Spirit. He wants that which we can know in this age to motivate us to live differently, to abide in Him. He wants our perspective to be an eternal one, so we will understand that the End-Times, though full of difficulty, hardship and suffering, will be but a second in time compared to the endless number of years we will drink from the fountain of the river of life in eternity.

The apostle John was given a glimpse of just how glorious our future will be. He spoke of this in 1 John 3:1-3. "It has not yet been revealed what we shall be." With these words he gave us that same glimpse, the same anticipation of our destiny as children of God. "…but we know that when He is revealed," John said with excitement, "we shall be like Him, for we shall see Him as He is." He used that insight to motivate his beloved friends to pursue what was real and eternal, and put aside worldly, temporary pursuits. Right now, Jesus, our Great Intercessor, is contending in Heaven for us to come to a place where we will do the same. He is asking that His Bride make the same shift in priorities. We know our loving God awaits us and in His presence we will find the fullness of joy (Ps. 16:11). God longs for us to begin now our new, eternal lives in Him and with Him. Because we have become so disconnected from our true identities as children of God and all that comes with that glorious distinction, we live far beneath our true nature and calling.

To reconnect to the awesome destiny that awaits us in the eternal age to come is to begin again. To be stirred in the deep places of our hearts by the grandeur and the splendor of what will constitute our "real" life, is to view our present life in this age in a different light. This book is meant to inspire people to begin a new journey. The path is truly an ancient one, but it has an eternal destination. Once the book is finished, that new life can begin. It must be a life dedicated to prayer, fasting, and the passionate study of the Word of God. It is these pursuits that will prepare us to navigate the trials of this life successfully and catapult us into the eternal calling of God.

Studying the End-Times is not meant to be a hobby, a past-time, a curious pursuit. It is meant to be a consuming journey into the knowledge of God to discover who He is and what He is like. It is meant to connect us with the realities of a life beyond this one, in a new world and a new age prepared for us from before the beginning of time. End-time passages are a gift that, if received, will equip us to live in radical obedience and abandon, not loving this world, which is passing away (1 John 2:15-17). "He who does the will of God abides forever" (1 John 2:17). What is the will of God? Ultimately, the will of God is for us to know Him. To let His will become your life's obsession is the most worthy of pursuits. To do so because you are living for the treasures of another age — "treasures in heaven" (Matt. 6:20-21). It's the final and best reason to study the End-Times: your heart is already somewhere else, and you are hungry to discover where it is.

END-TIMES FORUM

If you have questions about the End-Times or would like to dialogue with David Sliker and others on the subject, please go to our question and answer forum for the End-Times on the Onething Web site. You can discuss with others end-time Bible passages, ideas and concepts, as well as other related topics. Get ideas for resources, strategies to go deeper in study, connect with others who have a similar hunger to understand the End-Times and more! The address is *www.IHOP.org/onething.*

onething

Onething is more than a conference.

It is a ministry committed to seeing a great awakening in the Body of Christ as the hearts of men and women come alive to the true nature of God.

Onething is a young adult ministry based at the International House of Prayer in Kansas City, Missouri. We at Onething have a specific message and carry a mandate to call young adults to return to their primary purpose in this life: loving Jesus. We endeavor to assist young adults in walking out the first commandment to love the Lord with all of their hearts, minds, souls and strength and to pursue a wholehearted passion for Jesus.

Our desire is for the truth of the Man Jesus to pierce hearts, remove chains of bondage, open eyes to understanding, revive complacent hearts, and ultimately cause young adults to become wholehearted lovers of Jesus Christ.

**ONE THING HAVE I DESIRED, AND THAT WILL I SEEK ...
PSALM 27:4**

WHAT DO YOU DESIRE?

www.IHOP.org

THE FORERUNNER SCHOOL OF MINISTRY

Redefining Theological Education
Through Night and Day Prayer

Four Schools:
- School of Apostolic Preaching   Four-Year Program
- School of Worship and Prayer   Three-Year Program
- School of Healing and Prophecy   Two-Year Program
- School of Biblical Studies   Two-Year Program

One Academy:
- Forerunner Music Academy   Three-Year Program

Two Institutes:
- Joseph Company
- Apostolic Missions

CTEE:
- E-School – offering access to Video/Audio/Class Notes

Contact us:
12444 Grandview Road
Grandview, Missouri 64030
Phone: 816.763.0243
Fax: 816.763.0439
www.IHOP.org